Always Beginning

MAXINE KUMIN

Always Beginning

ESSAYS ON A LIFE IN POETRY

COPPER CANYON PRESS

Grateful acknowledgment is made to William Slater for the use of
"The House on the Ocean Near 10 Mile Creek" on the cover.

Copper Canyon Press is in residence under the auspices of the Centrum
Foundation at Fort Worden State Park in Port Townsend, Washington.
Centrum sponsors artist residencies, education workshops for Washington
State students and teachers, blues, jazz, and fiddle tunes festivals, classical
music performances, and The Port Townsend Writers' Conference.

LIBRARY OF CONGRESS CATALOGING-IN-PUBLICATION DATA

Kumin, Maxine, 1925–
Always beginning : essays on a life
in poetry / by Maxine Kumin.
p. cm.
ISBN 1-55659-141-1 (alk. paper)

1. Kumin, Maxine, 1925– 2. Poets, American – 20th century –
Biography. 3. Poetics. 4. Poetry. I. Title.

PS3521.U638 Z463 2000
811'.54 – DC21
00-009936
CIP

3 5 7 9 8 6 4 2
FIRST PRINTING

COPPER CANYON PRESS
Post Office Box 271
Port Townsend, Washington 98368
www.coppercanyonpress.org

ACKNOWLEDGMENTS

Many of these essays, some in slightly different form, have appeared or are forthcoming in the following publications:

"Recitations," *First Person Singular: Writers on Their Craft,* edited by Joyce Carol Oates, Ontario Review Press, 1983.

"Interstices," *The Leap Years: Women Reflect on Change, Loss, and Love,* edited by Mary Anne Maier and Joan Shaddox Isom. Beacon Press, 1999.

"Appreciation: The Selected Letters of Marianne Moore," *Prairie Schooner,* Winter, 1998.

"A Postcard from the Volcano," *Poets Reading: The Field Symposia,* edited by David Walker. Oberlin College Press, 1999.

"Swimming and Writing," *A Whole Other Ball Game,* edited by Joli Sandoz. Farrar, Straus & Giroux, 1999.

"Scrubbed Up and Sent to School," *Night Errands: How Poets Use Dreams,* edited by Roderick Townley. University of Pittsburgh Press, 1998.

"For Anne at Passover," *Jewish American Poetry: Poems, Commentary and Reflections,* edited by Jonathan Barron and Eric Murphy Selinger. © 2000 by the Trustees of Brandeis University, published by the University Press of New England.

"Beans," *My Favorite Plant: Writers and Gardeners on the Plants They Love,* edited by Jamaica Kincaid. Farrar, Straus, and Giroux, 1998.

"On 'A Shropshire Lad,'" *Touchstones: American Poets on a Favorite Poem,* edited by Robert Pack and Jay Parini. University Press of New England, 1995.

"Word for Word ('Poem for My Son')," *Introspections: American Poets on One of Their Own Poems,* edited by Robert Pack and Jay Parini. University Press of New England, 1997.

"Two Junes," *Creative Nonfiction* (Issue 7), 1996.

"October 4, 1995," *Green Mountains Review,* Fall/Winter 1996–97; Spring/Summer 1997.

"Josephine Jacobsen," *Poetry Society of America Bulletin,* Autumn, 1997.

"Pleasures: Excerpts from a June Journal," *Women's Review of Books,* Summer, 1998.

"Motherhood and Poetics," *New Writings on Motherhood and Poets,* edited by Patricia Dienstfrey and Brenda Hillman. University of California Press, 2000.

"First Loves," *Poetry Society of America Bulletin,* Spring 1998.

"Back to the Fairground: Mona Van Duyn," *Discovery and Reminiscence: Essays on the Poetry of Mona Van Duyn,* edited by Michael Burns. University of Arkansas Press, 1998.

"Gymnastics: The Villanelle," *An Exaltation of Forms* edited by Annie Finch and Katherine Varnes. University of Michigan Press, 2000.

"May, 1993," *The Writer's Journal,* edited by Sheila Bender, Dell Publishing, 1997.

Excerpt from "An Interview with Maxine Kumin," by Enid Shomer. *The Massachusetts Review,* Winter, 1996–97.

"Essay on Robert Frost," *Gone Into If Not Explained: Essays on Poems by Robert Frost,* edited by Greg Kuzma. The Best Cellar Press, 1976.

Contents

If the angel deigns to come, it will be because
you have convinced him, not by tears, but by
your humble resolve to be always beginning:
to be a beginner.

RAINER MARIA RILKE

Always Beginning

PART ONE

Excerpts from a June Journal

JUNE 20, 1995

A perfectly average ho-hum sort of day. My tone here is ironic: the elderly walk-behind Gravely tractor I've been begging my husband Victor to replace has seized up once again. After two trips to Concord for "parts" – mysterious bit-by-bit replacement of innards – it ran brilliantly for three days. Our once-in-a-while hired hand was to attack the back fields with it today, and today, of course, it refuses to turn over. So Rip is finishing the chain-sawing of the poplar pile, that untidy mountain of six-foot lengths of poplar tops left over from last winter's feeding of horses. Every November our hay and cordwood supplier, a local farmer, brings me two cords of fairly skinny poplar tops, useless for anything else, but ideal for debarking and toying with by equines. I can't remember where I learned this technique, but it provides roughage, relieves boredom, and keeps the horses from chewing great gaps in the fence boards all winter long. As soon as the first grass appears they disdain the logs. *Why are you feeding us trees? What do you take us for?* On the coldest winter nights I often awaken with pleasurable satisfaction to the hollow thock! thock! sound their teeth make gnawing on poplar. It approaches the gratification of hearing an infant just beginning to shake his rattle.

Since, like good Yankees, we must put everything to use, the idea is to cut the poplar pieces into stove-size chunks and stack them to burn in the fall, when a quick hot fire that doesn't last is just the thing to take the chill off the house. There is joy in a neatly stacked pile; providence brings its own kind of pleasure. Sawing wood is what we theoretically do in our spare time, or on a day when the tractor breaks down, or when it is drizzly, not raining hard enough to force one indoors, but too wet to mow.

I spent my usual hour in the garden this morning, papering and mulching my corn rows. The staid old *New York Times* has started using color illustrations in the *Book Review,* but I am relieved to read in *Organic Gardening* that these dyes are safe to use for bedding plants. I save my *Book Review*s most of the year as the width of the pages opened out fits perfectly between stalks. I mulch on top of the paper with spoiled hay sweepings, also saved all year from the barn floor, plus the occasional flakes of hay that clump together in a suspicious manner suggesting mold. Luckily, we encounter very little spoilage in the 600-odd bales of hay we feed each year.

I love getting up to the garden early, while the thrushes are singing their hearts out and a flurry of warblers can be seen high in the trees. Now that everything has leafed out, I have to rely on ear rather than eye to identify the rose-breasted grosbeak, cardinal, catbird, and so on. Squatting in the garden, sitting on the edge of one raised bed while I work on the next, is my serene and private time. While my hands are working my brain is also busy, ruminating, fantasizing, opening out like nasturtium buds.

A steadier rain is falling now. V. has gone faithfully out in the rain to scrub out and refill the bathtub in the Elysian Field for whatever horses spend the night there. He will eventually come in drenched, shuck his clothes, shower, find dry and equally tattered jeans and shirt, and tuck into an enormous lunch. Somehow he keeps his good humor in the teeth of the total frustration inanimate objects can breed in a person. I think he burned his fury out yesterday on this machine. I would have pitched it into the gully years ago. And now, magically! the welcome roar of the motor! But of course it's too wet to mow now, anyway.

JUNE 26

Mammoth mowings have taken place and will, it is hoped, continue, until the last of our fifteen acres of forage pasture have been brushed out down to the fence lines. My heart leaps up at the sight of tidily mowed pasture, green and sweet for the grazing. In my former life I am convinced I was one of the herd, head down in the grasses, mesmerized by appetite and instinct. How I love my living landscape! The rest of our 170 acres consists of craggy forest, granite outcroppings and punishing hills. Deep woods bring their own sort of fulfillment, but strict fields gladden me more.

Our grandson Yann is with us for four days until Andover summer school commences, and he is happy to mow extensively for four dollars an hour, delighting in the fact that he is now deemed old enough to operate serious machinery. He arrived with his head shaved almost to the crown, a little going-away present proffered by one of his soccer teammates. It is sweetly pathetic to see the warring impulses in a fourteen-and-a-half-year-old male. Macho is at odds with sensitive, empathetic human. Intellect struggles with pop cult, rap, sitcom, etc. Coming-of-age sexual feelings war with terror of same.

Not much improvement in the area of responsibility. Both his wallet and his sunglasses went through the wash this morning; he said it was okay, as it had happened before. But this is an age when an inner voice reciting *me me me* takes precedence over all else. Wet towels are abandoned in midthought; lamps are turned on and forgotten forever. Our son Danny drove to Boston to meet Yann's flight and will conduct him to Andover on the appointed day: Danny, who was possibly the most irresponsible unresponsive alienated adolescent in history, now recast as Mr. Straight-Arrow Father and Husband. It is delicious to see genes transmitted from generation to generation. And it tickles me to watch Yann and his much younger cousin Noah performing that all-American-boy ritual of shooting baskets into the hoop mounted on Danny's garage, taking their part in the continuum.

JUNE 28

To my surprise and delight, I've written a new poem, the first in several months. It came up out of the void, built from a few oracular notes taken weeks, even months apart, scribbled on notepads from different motels, one in Washington, D.C., another in Missouri, as well as some lines I jotted while I was teaching in Southern California. I've put it through about five drafts now and feel pretty confident that I've got it right, particularly as a new finale and a title arrived unbespoke while I was typing the last draft. There is no pleasure comparable to the secret pleasure of a new and gratifying poem, a poem that feels complete and without problems, a poem that emerged mysteriously, blindly growing its own connective tissue as it evolved. If I'm lucky I may find another new poem to chew on, as one poem tends to beget another. Howard Nemerov always said that his poems surfaced in groups, like cluster headaches, so I will try to be patiently attentive.

JUNE 29

The month is drawing to a close, the days are growing shorter – already! – we have not swum yet in our magical three-quarter-acre pond, so it can't be full summer, yet the garden is safely in hand, houseguests are beginning to sprout as they always do at this season, and I have the beginnings of a suntan. We are still single-mindedly pursuing the same goals of fecund garden, safe pastures, healthy horses. I've begun a second poem, which resists me, but I think it will eventually come right.

Yann appears to be thriving at Andover, to everyone's relief. He's playing piano in a jazz band, has found a tennis partner, and loves his course in speech and debate, where they're doing a moot court. I paraphrase Bernard Shaw, who said somewhere that youth is a wonderful thing; what a pity to waste it on children. But I wouldn't miss Yann's growing up for anything.

The actual date of our anniversary has come and gone (yesterday) and V. is now telling everyone that we've embarked on our second half-century together. We had a perfectly ordinary day: he mowed, I mowed; he took his horse for a longish hack, I picked snow peas and organized dinner, celebratory with son, daughter-in-law, their six-year-old son Noah, and her father and stepmother and aunt, an event made special with lobster and a salad of three kinds of our own lettuce. I even found space to work on the recalcitrant poem a while.

I am grateful for every such ordinary day, knowing that these will draw to a close somewhere beyond our seeing. I hope to go on picking vegetables, pulling bindweed out of the fields (the recalcitrant poem's subject), enjoying the birds, the dogs, even our elderly cat, whose last season this likely will be. I had a long long-distance conversation with my friend in Bucks County whose kitten this cat was twenty-one years ago. At age eighty-two my friend is still breeding her mares, tending three stallions, living in dishevelment but with ongoing zest, and is now writing her memoir. I know it will be a fascinating account from her pearly childhood on Park Avenue through the several marriages, the eternal commitment to dogs and horses and any wandering critter that crosses her path. I admire her tenacity and wit and hope she can go on doing what she's doing as long as she wishes. We have a considerable history together, beginning in 1976 when she showed up in one of my classes at Princeton with her eccentric and quite extraordinary poems. And I suppose a tribute to friendship is a good way to close out this month's entries, a tribute to enduring relationships in general, to the loyalty that underlies them. Going on is, after all, the ultimate pleasure of our lives.

Beans

Long ago in suburban Boston, when I was but a dilettante gardener content with a flat of petunias and a few commercially started tomato plants, I first came upon Thoreau's essay "The Bean-Field." *Walden* was part of the core curriculum of freshman English at Tufts University, where I was a part-time instructor, and although my acquaintance with the genus *Phaseolus* was nil, my job required me to pay close attention to the text.

"What shall I learn of beans or beans of me?" Henry David asks. His real concern in this chapter is not with matters of cultivation but with sensuous joys – walking barefoot, observing birds, admiring the emerging wild blackberries. But what overtook him as he hoed his rows was the intrinsic pleasure of his labor, of "making the earth say beans instead of grass."

Forty years later, slave of my garden, I have grown intimate with beans. They are my stars, my best producers, my most versatile charmers. The average bean of our acquaintance began in South America and was an early-explorer export to Europe in the mid-1600s. Horticulturists have been experimenting with and improving the basic cultivar ever since Gregor Johann Mendel unriddled the secrets of garden peas. The lowly bean comes in a surprising array of possibilities, from compact plants barely a foot high to Jack-and-the-Beanstalk giants. There are half-runners that extend obediently only a foot or so, real runners that wrap around four-foot stakes, and pole beans for which the sky is the limit.

I regret that my life will not be long enough to try them all, but I've done some experimenting. In the bush-bean department I've raised Provider, Seville, skinny French flageolet, and flat Romanos planted in triangular clusters down the three-foot-wide row. Of pole beans, I've enabled yellow and green Kentucky Wonders to hurl themselves up chicken wire or, more recently, fish netting that washed ashore on Cape Cod, where we found great clumps of it on the deserted beach on an autumn vacation.

This year, I am raising pole limas with delicate yellow blossoms that will likely not pod up to bear more than a meal or two though I started them indoors in April, cosseted them through May on the glassed-in front porch, and set them out in the garden on Memorial Day. I have long depended on purple tepee beans, tougher but very hardy, that come to fruition a little later than the green beans and turn a gratifying green when blanched.

I have not yet said scarlet runner beans, whose showy flowers attract hummingbirds, or the hyacinth bean, which was favored by Thomas Jefferson, who had an elaborate arbor for them constructed at Monticello. Scarlet runners and hyacinths both produce edible beans even though they are mostly grown for their flowers. Shelling-out kinds of climbers like Jacob's Cattle beans, Bert Goodwin, black turtle, and cranberry beans will happily twine up any support, including cornstalks, where they will flourish without impeding the ripening ears.

I've tried soybeans, edible in their green phase or allowed to dry for shelling out, but found them no improvement over standard green-bean varieties. One year I undertook to raise fava beans with their purple-spotted white flowers, which grow on the same time schedule as peas, favoring cool weather and good moisture. They are a thick, showy plant and would like to be staked as they otherwise want to flop over as they grow. The penny-size beans are a penance to dislodge from their thick and somewhat prickly pods, which form along the length of the stalk; I didn't know at the time that one can blanch them for a minute or two and overcome this difficulty. Some people of Mediterranean heritage are quite allergic to favas. But this bean isn't a bean after all. It's a vetch, an herb of the genus *Vicia faba* that originated in western Asia.

Then there are adzuki beans of Asian extraction, grown mostly for their edible sprouts, and the asparagus, or yard-long bean, which produces winged pods after its cinnamon-red flowers have gone by. There is the rattlesnake bean, a climber that is bright green with purple stripes, and the horticultural bean, one of which, the Scarlet Beauty Elite, is touted by Pinetree Garden Seeds of Maine as the shell bean that "has outsold Jacob's Cattle beans at the Buckfield General Store," the seeds of which "are amongst the loveliest we have seen, elongated with beautiful shades of purplish brown and beige."

Pinetree further says, of Jacob's Cattle, "What Saturday night Bean Supper would be complete without Jacob's Cattle and its remarkable effects on the digestive tract?" (Reading seed catalogs is a wonderful indoor sport!) This bean is sometimes called Trout or Dalmatian bean; New Englanders treasure it because it dries earlier than any other variety and in our short summers this is a useful attribute.

A friend loaned me a colorful British book on giant vegetables. Following instructions in the text it is now possible to grow beans over twenty inches long (they will be tough, the author warns). Apparently the cultivation of giant veggies, which began among the Brits, has become a competitive sport, slower than cricket and perhaps more suspenseful. At horticultural shows worldwide such entries are scrupulously inspected and measured. Prizes are given. A gentleman in North Carolina achieved a winning runner bean forty-eight inches long.

I must say that stretching nature to its limits holds no fascination for me; indeed, I was somewhat horrified to read directions for straightening a bent bean after harvesting. You are directed to tie this miscreant as straight as possible at three-inch intervals to a strip of wood, wrap the whole package in a damp towel, and leave it alone to think the matter over for twenty-four hours. By then, the bean will have grown somewhat more supple and can be pulled out to its full length. Doesn't this sound like vegetable torture?

Almost any old beans can be grown for the seeds inside the pods, much as we grow English, or shelling-out, peas. Even unintentionally forgotten beans, weary beans you didn't get around to picking in time, will yield bean seeds that are delicious young, especially when braised with garlic and minced onion.

Dried, they can be displayed in glass jars until the snowy February day on which you decide to make a thick bean soup.

Some modest planning ahead is required. Dried beans need to soak overnight before going into the cooking pot along with everything else you have on hand. An all-day simmer fills the house with a tantalizing aroma worth, as they say, half the candle. By this time it may be blizzarding and the power may have gone out so that you will need all the candles you have providently stored up. But if you're an addicted vegetable gardener you develop this sort of storing-up personality: dried beans in jars, herbs in the cupboard, blanched vegetables enough to feed a battalion down cellar in the freezer.

Pests aren't much of a problem on beans in my garden. The dread Japanese beetle will move on from the raspberry patch to attack the uppermost leaves of pole beans late in the season. I handpick these copper-backed beasts and shake them off into a can filled with soapy water. Growing some sweet peas alongside beans encourages pollinating insects, I am told, and these in turn should discourage the evil kind. I am a great advocate of spray made from the Indian neem tree, now certified as safe for edibles as well as flowers and shrubs. It does not interfere with the action of the beneficials, those insects, like parasitic wasps, that interrupt the reproductive cycle of the invaders.

I confess nothing looks prettier to me than a well-tended flourishing vegetable garden. Raised beds, mown or mulched walkways, an attractive fence all around impose the discipline and order that are in short supply in my somewhat chaotic life. Once, I didn't know beans about beans. Now, I am a bean counter and proud of it.

June 1, 1991: Sleeping Late

Delicious to lie somewhere between sleep and wakefulness over-hearing the judiciously useful movements toward dailiness downstairs. Victor tousling the dogs, the squeak of the back door opening, the scrabble sound of toenails flying over pea stone toward the barn to terrorize Abra and Cadabra, the serene cats. The crunch of Victor's footsteps a few minutes later, the low-key nickers the broodmare makes, in her stall all night as we approach foaling time, happy to be served her morning ration of hay and sweet feed. I listen to his yodeling for the two other horses, turned out in the nearest pasture but with access to the open area under the barn. No sound. Lately, it's been so buggy they've stayed in the motel lobby most of the night, but apparently they are just now wandering in of their own accord. (Motel lobby is the name we've given the open area, once a cow-manure pit, under the barn.) The gliding sounds of latches opening, closing, feed being apportioned to receptive little nickers. Horses all stabled, footsteps again, up over the gravel, up and up to the pasture above the house, where the politically correct ponies, Justice and Independence, are spending the summer, alternating grazing with resting in the big run-in shed. They're too fat to require any grain, but each gets a token handful and a cursory look-over for any cuts or bruises that might have taken place overnight. Footsteps returning.

Now I do a little dozing, aware under the thin shawl that divides sleep from wakefulness of chickadee, oriole, rose-breasted grosbeak, and goldfinch territorial announcements. A sharp clatter of kibble into two dog dishes, the complaint of the coffee mill grinding beans. It's an old hand-turned mill we brought back from Amsterdam twenty years ago. Now I sink back into real slumber, secure in the knowledge that Someone Else is in charge, the day has begun without me and no harm has befallen.

Tonight, our first wild mushrooms of the season, two good handfuls of coral, which I found this morning on a rotting water bar in the upper pasture. Usually coral is such a pain to clean that I pass it by, but this bunch was free of pine needle duff and stood up sprightly from the dead wood it was growing on. We're eating our own lettuces and spinach now, and some young Chinese mustard greens as well.

Also, I noticed a young male rose-breasted grosbeak on the feeder just outside the kitchen window. He sat there, all dotted and dashed with his youthful plumage, and in the middle of his chest a pale pink splotch emerging. It seems awfully early for fledglings. But then I encountered a nascent tomato the size of a pea on my boldest Oregon Spring plant. Does this mean edible tomatoes before August? If so, we are probably in for it – the climate of Virginia arriving in New Hampshire in our lifetime.

The writer in me submerges at this season. My head is full of details and consequences. I need to put up some chive blossom vinegar this week, while the blooms are at their pungent best. It is clearly time to cut an armload of tarragon to dry, before it overruns everything else in my sprawling, haphazard herbal bed. And the annual mowing mowing mowing, trying to keep abreast of the late spring growth so that in midsummer there will still be a flush of good grass coming in the pastures. I must hunt up the extra-strength Betadine, Boomer's old soft leather halter, the intercom that Victor sets up to work from barn to bedroom, but which I can never seem to rely on. After a night or two of lying awake misinterpreting every squeak and rustle, I will be ready to move down to the sawdust bin in the barn to await the birthing.

June 16, 1991: Final Foal

Five days after our foal was born, and this is the first time I've been able to direct myself to the desk. Born at eleven PM on June 11, only a little while after I'd settled into my sleeping bag, not yet drifted off, not exactly expecting anything, as the actual due date was the 15th, but kept awake or jostled from a doze by a cat or cats, then hearing the rush of waters. Raised on one elbow to peer over the stall wall at Boomer, found her lying down, recognized it was her amniotic fluid rushing out. There seemed to be an awful lot of it, more than I'd heard in any of the other labors. Spoke softly – too softly, he didn't hear me – into the intercom to Victor: "Victor, Boomer's in labor. Bring the Betadine." No response. Slipped on shoes, raced up to house, opened door, spoke same words loudly, rushed back to barn.

Boomer now beginning to push. Sac, blue, lumpish, beginning to bulge. She was, I thought, too close to the wall, but before I could panic she got up, repositioned, went down again. I saw something sticking out though still enclosed in membrane: a leg? Yes, now another similar stick. God, let these not be hind legs, prayed this nonbeliever. Now the unmistakable lump of a head, still tightly cauled. Boomer not straining, going about this calmly, methodically, resting, then pushing.

I slipped the latch, went in, knelt down, but before I could tear the sac open it tore on its own and a real head emerged, with open eyes; then a muzzle opened and breathed. Before I could even think about it, she had passed the rest of the body. The hind legs trailed out, like afterthoughts. Boomer got up at once – *much too soon!* I wanted to tell her – but she was up and began licking her baby. She tongued it all over quite gently, spoke to it very softly, and it very softly answered, still coiled in fetal position.

At this moment I realized Victor had arrived, Betadine in hand. Of course I got it all over me as well as all over the underbelly of the foal – I still didn't know what gender it was – as I struggled to cover the navel stump. Getting the stump painted right away is high priority, as this is the easiest entry site for bad bacteria. No matter how many times I have done this, I do it clumsily, messily. I realized my hands were shaking.

Boomer was now standing there dripping, no, practically raining blood. It looked like too much blood, so I called the vet, got the answering service; they in turn woke the vet, who, to my misfortune, was the male vet in the triumvirate, and quite obviously ticked off at having been so rudely roused. He told me that if she had torn something the blood would be gushing out, not just dripping fast.

She continued to drip for the next twenty minutes; then it tapered off. Now I started searching the foal's undercarriage for a vital piece of male equipment. This was our ninth foal and we'd only had two colts so far. It gradually dawned on me that no matter how hard I looked there was to be no penis. Another filly! A miracle. All this by flashlight.

Now we decided both baby and mare were alert enough to tolerate electricity, so we turned on the overhead lights. Baby began to try to stand. This endearing and pathetic behavior full of staggers and tumbles took almost half an hour. Finally she was up, looking bewildered. We thought she should nurse. Boomer started backing away, she loved her baby but couldn't bear to have her on a teat. Same problem she had with her last foal. We put a lead shank on the mare, started edging baby to udder, but babe was too tall, or not hungry enough, or not smart enough to get her head under and angled *up*. After what seemed like hours of this effort, I went into the house and dialed my horse helper Wendy. She picked up on the sixth ring, knew immediately what was happening, said, "I'll be right there." And was, as fast as she could drive from her farm to ours, fifteen minutes at high speed.

Victor fetched the two-by-four to fit in the slot we used last time. He set it up and we eased Boomer into position. Now she couldn't swivel to avoid the foal; still, the foal couldn't or wouldn't fasten on. Wendy milked out about five cc into a cup and syringed it down the foal's throat so at least she would ingest some of the initial colostrum. Colostrum contains antibodies that are essential for the baby's health.

It was ten minutes of two in the morning before the baby got an actual first suck. We were exhausted. Victor went back to bed, I went back on top of the sawdust pile. Wendy set up a lawn chair in the stall and said she would read a magazine so as to be available if the foal couldn't nurse on her own. She and I chatted intermittently, I dozed off mercifully. At first light – 4:30 – Wendy went home; I sat in the chair. Boomer was now readily accepting her foal as her tight udder eased. At 6.30 I woke Victor, he came down and removed the board that had confined Boomer. Meanwhile I had given the foal a Fleet enema, standard postdelivery procedure here, and I'd given Boomer a hot bran mash sweetened with molasses. She had passed the placenta, which appeared intact; her own plumbing was in working order. I went to bed in my own bed, Victor sat outside the stall, sipping coffee.

Today I am watching a five-day-old foal gallop catty-corner across the paddock at top, which is to say heart-stopping, speed. She has an enormous stride and looks very strong, though still spindly. She is almost an exact replica of her mother, mouse dun with a dorsal stripe, and black points. A lovely little Arab-dished face. We've named her Booms Hallelujah – the registry does not permit apostrophes – to be known as Lu. Our final filly, I promised Victor. I think I am ready to give up having babies and concentrate on bringing this last one to a mature state of grace.

Journal Entry, PoBiz, Texas

The pobiz profession is wondrous strange. On a free Sunday morning during an arduous gig in central Texas, Chester Critchfield, a retired biologist who bounces along jauntily on the balls of his sneakered feet, conveys me on a guided tour of the native flora and fauna. An enthusiast who would rather spend an hour watching a flower open than chase a golf ball across the ubiquitous greens, Chester is vividly at one with his environment. Behind his house where the land drops down to the creek he has excavated a sizable pond, lined it with limestone bricks, and stocked it with Japanese carp exotically striped and stippled orange, black, and white. Several ugly catfish patrol the bottom and a healthy school of tilapia rise to snap at the pellets he broadcasts over the surface. Tilapia, he informs me, are the biblical fish of the Sea of Galilee. He thinks they and the carp would do well in my sheep-pasture fire pond, a saucer some fifty feet in diameter, possibly eight feet deep at the center.

As we cross the adjoining meadow I see my first loggerhead shrike under Chester's tutelage; it's a savage little bird of prey that impales its quivering catch on thorns, then retrieves and devours them at leisure. I had always expected a shrike to be bigger than a blue jay, at least. It makes up in ferocity for what it lacks in stature.

We drive out to a huge Thoroughbred breeding farm where Chester has made arrangements for a guided tour. Ken Quirk, the resident vet, is one of the most gracious hosts I've come across in these often sterile and forbidding establishments. We arrive at an easy rapport in spite of the hard night he's been through – a leased mare, bred last summer and then sent home to her owner who failed to have her ultrasounded early in the pregnancy, was returned to them a few weeks ago for supervised foaling. Last night she delivered full-term twins, in itself a rarity, as the mare's uterus seldom provides an eleven-month-long hospitable environment for twins. The filly is near death, sedated with Valium to control her seizures. She is a "wobbler," or "dummy foal," a condition caused by inflammation of brain tissue. They are trying to reduce the swelling with DMSO infusions, but it doesn't look good. The colt has a better chance. He's been up, with assistance. He has a sucking reflex but is not yet able to swallow. Both are being fed four ounces of colostrum from the mother, milked out and delivered via stomach tube every two hours. The vet's heroic measures put our own dozen travails with dams and foals into perspective. Of course I am fascinated.

One hundred forty-three bred mares here, the newest still in open pens under a high roof, which provides good ventilation. But with so many so close, there's a higher incidence of infection than, say, on the family farm. With us, predelivery precautions consist of taking out the old bedding down to sand and gravel, liming the area, and then rebedding. When the mare actually gives birth – or shortly before she does so, if we're alert to it – we switch from sawdust to straw, to reduce the possibility of a newborn inhaling sawdust particles and ammonia fumes from the urine. One of our mares, a greedy old lady, *eats* straw, which complicates things a bit. We've sat out a few tough nights with mares whose distended udders made them reluctant to give suck but we've never – so far – had a bacterial or any other postnatal infection.

It's still showery and cool here although spring is well advanced. The redbuds have finished flowering and are putting out new leaves. Older colts and their mothers are turned out on pasture in groups of six or eight. These old-time broodmares coexist comfortably. Fifteen stallions cover this herd: retired stakes winners, sons and latter-day descendants of Seattle Slew and Native Dancer. The stallion's life is far from enviable, however. All of them are confined to box stalls as we tour, though Dr. Quirk says they are usually turned out. It's Sunday, and Sunday is a down day at this farm. One stalwart morose stud is wearing a muzzle. We can see where he tears himself up biting in frustration. He covered eighty mares last year, which seems an extraordinary figure. It would be a kindness to castrate him and let him have an outdoor life free of his gonads, but he's a moneymaker.

They raise ostriches here too, but the birds are setting now and can't be viewed. A fertile egg is worth as much as $1,500 – so much for any fantasies of breeding ostriches! Tilapia sound more reasonable.

Two days later I am driven in a stretch limousine, complete with liquor bar and TV, back to the airport for a predawn departure. A first for me, the limo, but I chafe, thinking how wasteful and ostentatious it is.

I loved the carp. They live, Chester told me, as much as ninety years. You too, Chester. Be well.

Notes from My Journal, Kyoto, December 1984

There are 172 members of the Emily Dickinson Society in Japan. Emily is revered by professors of literature; they see her poetry as a forgivably loose kind of haiku. Can an American writer bridge the cultural gap? Can a poet write haikus in English? Tankas? If so, why? These and other issues arise over dinner. I have a wonderful consecutive interpreter. He goes like the wind even though he has never interpreted for a poet before, scribbling notes in Japanese and English on a thick lined pad. I find I have to make notes, too, to remember what I want to say next, when I must pause frequently to let him deal with the material. Afterward we are full of mutual congratulations. He confesses that he dreaded this assignment, afraid it would be technical, beyond his grasp, but now he says he feels a deep affection for poetry. The supreme compliment!

The temples are as orange as Howard Johnson's. The plastic mock-ups of meals outside the meanest restaurant are meant to leap the language barrier, but since the foods themselves are unfamiliar, the displays raise more questions than they answer. Can this be pickled sea-worm? How closely these things resemble testicles. The braided hanks are a vegetable. And so on.

It is only five days since our Japan Airlines plane blew a tire on takeoff from Bangkok, skidded to a halt on the far end of the runway, and caught fire. I haven't been able to get rid of the sounds the little flight attendants made as they ran ululating up and down the cabin, in terror for their mortal souls. The smoke was not very thick but the danger of an explosion felt real enough; I remember turning to V. and saying, "I'm glad we're together..." And I never want to go down a yellow escape chute again. After they finally got one open at our end of the plane, people were very orderly, not at all like sheep crowding to go into the dip they fear. By the time we got to the top of the slide, there were rescuers in huge white (asbestos?) space suits stationed at the bottom. They caught us as we flew down, stood us on our feet, and urged, "Run!" in English. I remember I was struck by that. If you don't get caught by people at the foot of the slide, chances are excellent that you will break both ankles. And then the creamy sequence of a day spent at Rama Gardens, like an R and R center, sitting by the pool, cruising the splendid buffet, dozing in a suite of rooms, getting up the courage to reembark that same evening. I am cured of international travel.

PART TWO

Interstices

Victor and I met through mutual friends on a blind date on the 19th of April 1945. It was Patriots' Day, a holiday previously unknown to me, but a significant one in Massachusetts. Schools and many businesses close in honor of the midnight ride of Paul Revere; tradition has established that the annual Boston Marathon be run on that day. (Since 1969, Patriots' Day has been celebrated on the third Monday in April, making it a moveable feast.)

In common with many of his classmates who had gone off to serve in World War II, Victor missed graduation. He had been granted a Harvard diploma at midsemester in 1943. Now he was a staff sergeant in the Army, a rather unprepossessing rank in my eyes. All three of my brothers were officers. Home on a ten-day furlough from a place in New Mexico that I had never heard of – Los Alamos – he was extremely vague about what he did there, though he did tell me that he had been in infantry training in Alabama and got transferred. I didn't know enough to ferret out the mystery.

A serious history and lit major, a dean's list Radcliffe junior, I was wearing, according to the custom of the time, my quasi-boyfriend's Navy ensign's gold bar pinned to my sloppy-joe sweater. I had been going out with – "seeing," we called it – my Navy man for three years, ever since we met as counselors at adjoining summer camps in the Berkshires. He was blond and rather good-looking. His manners were impeccable. A man of the world, he had slid through Harvard with gentleman's Cs but felt that his future was assured. My mother doted on him. I was grateful when he shipped out on his destroyer to shepherd convoys crossing the Atlantic. The chemistry between us was wrong; I felt uneasily that I was being pressured to make a commitment to someone who was nothing more than a friendly date.

Victor and I saw each other for five days in a row. There was then, and continues to be, no explanation for our instant and mutual attraction. Looking at a snapshot taken that following summer, I see how darling we were, he lean and saturnine in a white T-shirt and baggy khakis snugged tight with a belt, I in a sexy striped bathing suit and smoking a very sophisticated cigarette. My shoulder-length hair is wavy and dips over one eye in the style of a long-forgotten movie star. There's something raffish, sexually provocative and at the same time vulnerable, about the two kids in that photo. We look as though we belong together; in fact, we are flaunting it. But did we have any idea of the long marriage we were letting ourselves in for?

During those five days in April 1945 I think Victor came to some of my classes, for even in my newly besotted state, I wasn't about to cut any lectures; once, I remember, he came to the dorm for dinner. Dinners back then were formal affairs. We had to wear skirts, we stood behind our chairs until the housemother entered and took her seat and I think we even said a few words of grace, a practice I have come to resent, almost to detest. Why do agnostics and atheists have to pay lip service to belief?

Biddies, for that was how the mostly Irish maids were known, served each table. The biddies were our dear friends and confidantes; they cleaned our rooms and mooned over the framed pictures on our bureaus and mothered us in ways that college students today would find quaint if not politically reprehensible. My special one, Helen, winked her approval as she proffered Victor his plate. We went to the ballet – God knows where he found money for tickets – we went to the zoo. We walked around the Boston Gardens and Beacon Hill.

For us, April was definitely not the cruelest month. I can't remember if the magnolias were in bud on Commonwealth and Marlborough, but they should have been. We sat in the darkest bar in Boston, in the old Lafayette Hotel, and nursed our drinks for hours at a time. I could make a sloe-gin fizz, the only thing I could stand the taste of, last half the night.

"I'm going to marry you," my soldier said. "Come meet my family just in case, no strings attached, but I'm going to marry you." I seemed to have lost whatever mind of my own I had once had. We drove up to Salem to meet his sister, a child psychologist, and her pediatrician husband. I went to the train station to see Victor off and he introduced me to his mother, who had also come to South Station to say her farewells. I was too shy to kiss her son good-bye in her presence. What a different world that was! His brother was at sea in the Pacific theater, a five-year stint, so meeting him would have to wait until the war's end. (At our wedding, Victor wore his brother's navy trousers. Two inches too short, two inches too big in the waist, they were the closest he could come to formal black attire. He also wore Jerry's black shoes, a size too big.)

There ensued a marathon of letter writing. We wrote to each other daily for over a year, a ritual broken briefly in June when I traveled by train to Amarillo, Texas, and Victor hitchhiked down – across? – from New Mexico. I had an uncle in the Air Force who was stationed in Amarillo. His daughter had some sort of clerical position on the post and I had come, it was announced, for a visit. After this, I was to travel to Little Rock, Arkansas, where my lieutenant-colonel brother and his wife had a new baby and needed any help they could get. My brother was finally stateside after going through the Africa campaign and the landing on the Italian boot. He had guarded German POWs and stormed Monte Cassino, but seemed dazed by fatherhood. What I knew about baby-tending fell far short of what I knew, for instance, about the Nicene Creed or the Spenserian sonnet, but it was thought I could learn to make myself useful.

Did my parents have any foreknowledge of this rendezvous in the Southwest? I think not. But my uncle, on learning that Victor and I could extend our two-day visit by forty-eight hours if he went back to Los Alamos and signed in, arranged for a hotel room in Albuquerque. This uncle was on the lam from his marriage; he was having an affair with a Wac captain. Clearly he thought all romantic desires deserved to be gratified. A free spirit, he had been an underage sailor in the First World War. It is a mystery how he wormed his way as an officer into the Second and a further mystery how he inveigled a hotel room in an overcrowded town on a weekend full of military on overnight passes.

We traveled to Alby by bus across the desert; the bus broke down around midnight and the passengers all disembarked to lie on the still-warm sand and admire the cactus roses in bloom under a bright canopy of Western sky. Victor got back late to the base and was rewarded with a week's KP. I entrained for Little Rock and two weeks of baby perambulation and housekeeping.

We didn't see each other again until Thanksgiving. In what we now regarded as "our" bar of the Lafayette Hotel we agreed to become formally engaged and hastily arranged a trip to Philadelphia so that Victor could meet my family. "What would you do if I said no?" my father asked when he asked for my hand. "I guess I'd marry her anyway," Victor replied. The engagement ring (chosen by my mother – I had no interest in it) wiped out his savings. Twenty years later, the diamond fell out of its setting somewhere on a bridle path while I was snapping overhanging branches as we rode along. I didn't notice the bare setting until that evening. Perhaps some millennia from now, its glint will catch the eye of a being who will take it back to the lair as an esoteric prize.

In December of that year, I elected to stay in Cambridge and work on my undergraduate honors thesis rather than go back to Philadelphia for the holidays. Rooms were made available at the Harvard Divinity School for those of us who had early February due dates for our magna opera. I had barely settled in to work when Victor arrived on an unexpected furlough. The water pipes at Los Alamos had frozen in an unusual cold snap and the Army had shipped several thousands of soldiers and scientists home until they could be repaired. What to do? I had a serious thesis to write.

Victor took charge. He came over each morning at eight with coffee and goodies and then absented himself all day. I read and scribbled diligently in my monk's cell, earning my release from drudgery on the dot of five, when Victor reappeared. On the stroke of midnight he returned me to my appointed task. By the time our holiday together had ended, my thesis was nearly finished, reinforcing my already ingrained Jewish-Calvinist work ethic.

Just after graduation in June of 1946, a scant three weeks after he was mustered out of the Army, Victor and I were married at the Warwick Hotel in Philadelphia in an elaborate ceremony staged entirely by my mother. It was to be a formal wedding, complete with Lohengrin and bridesmaids, unlimited champagne and platters of shrimp. We combed the city for a white dinner jacket to go with Victor's borrowed pants. Civilian clothes were all but unobtainable in that first postwar year, but he finally found a vintage number in Boston at Hirsch's Haberdashery on Massachusetts Avenue. I wore a satin bridal gown that had been worn before me by all three of my tiny sisters-in-law. A creative seamstress had altered it to fit me by changing the scoop neckline to an off-the-shoulder one and dropping the waist to hip height. I wore white ballet slippers; even so, the dress did not quite reach the desired floor-length.

That elaborate charade behind us, we honeymooned in a borrowed farmhouse about twenty miles north of the little town of Warner, a locus that became the inspiration for our move twenty-some years later to New Hampshire.

In the early days of the war, Victor had worked for a year and a half at the Woods Hole Oceanographic Institute conducting underwater explosions under the guidance of one of his Harvard professors. He had planned to go into the naval Air Force and said as much to E. Bright Wilson. "That's crazy!" Wilson exploded. "You'll be a dead hero. Come to Woods Hole and *really* help the war effort." But the Army drafted him despite several high-level pleas to have him deferred. Sent off to undergo grueling basic training in the infantry, he was within days of being shipped overseas to fight in the Battle of the Bulge when he was snatched out of Alabama. Under sealed orders he was escorted to the train and eventually arrived at the Los Alamos facility. There, to his astonishment, he discovered a dozen former Woods Hole colleagues who had mysteriously disappeared one by one during his tenure, and at least one Harvard professor who had also gone missing the same way.

Because all military personnel were guaranteed reemployment at the last position held, we returned to Woods Hole after the war, where Victor had rented an apartment for thirty-five dollars a month in the old U.S. Bureau of Fisheries building. Seals barked outside our window. Waves lapped the pilings and lulled us to sleep. We had two rooms, one of which contained a sink, an ancient electric stove, and an icebox. The ice had to be replenished every other day but the iceman never showed up on Mondays as he was sleeping off a hangover. On Mondays I rode my bike to the fish market and cadged a chunk of ice to bring home in my bike basket.

In his haste to find a place for us to live and his elation over the reasonable rent, Victor had not noticed that the apartment lacked a bathroom. We shared a communal one with several bachelors up one flight and down a long outdoor corridor. I was the only woman in the building, but the dormitory-style bathroom was mine from nine AM till five. The rest of the time, Victor accompanied me and stood guard outside the door.

Except for the lack of our own indoor amenity, the apartment suited us perfectly. It was a great way to start off our marriage. Since I had little to do except learn how to iron shirts, I began to write in secret the poems I had abandoned when I matriculated at Radcliffe. But creative writing was not held in high esteem at that time. Who knew that a thousand MFA programs coast to coast were to come? It was felt that writing their own stories and poems deflected students from the serious business of accruing knowledge.

In Woods Hole, Victor came home for lunch every day; his lab was literally within shouting distance. We swam or played tennis most evenings before supper, and took the ferry to Martha's Vineyard frequently to spend weekends with various college friends whose families had cottages in Menemsha. Meat rationing was still in effect; we fished for many of our dinners. K.C. – Kung-Chi Wang – an engineer from MIT who was to marry one of my closest college chums, came down from his summer job in Providence quite regularly to play tennis and show us how to deal with the dozens of puffers we caught off the wharf. He filleted them expertly, extracting from the tail of this otherwise poisonous fish the one choice tidbit that he stir-fried in whiskey and soy sauce.

Those three months provided the carefree foreground our marriage needed. Once back in Boston, housing was expensive and hard to find. There were career decisions to make. After a few false starts, Victor signed on as a process engineer with the Kendall Company in Walpole. Instead of atomic bombs, Kendall manufactured tampons and diapers. We moved six times that first year, from a one-roomer in the Back Bay to the top floor of what we later discovered was a fancy whorehouse in Brookline, and finally settled in one of those two-bedroom garden apartment housing developments that were mushrooming in rings around the big cities.

We were followed from place to place by the FBI, who interviewed our neighbors about our habits and practices and occasionally interviewed me on the pretext of inquiring about some unknown, nonexistent neighbor. David Greenglass had been in Victor's unit at Los Alamos; the Rosenberg case was about to blow open.

By then, I had gone back to Harvard to earn my master's degree in comparative literature and quickly completed the required credits. Hugely pregnant with my first child, I flunked the Latin exam, for which I was underprepared (the French exam was easy). Harry Levin, who had been my tutor during my senior year, interceded for me on grounds of impending motherhood and the committee agreed to award the degree so long as I was not planning to go on for a PhD. Levin was a wonderfully generous mentor. He oversaw my undergraduate honors thesis, grandiloquently titled "Amorality and the Protagonist in the Novels of Stendhal and Dostoyevsky," and never flinched at its pretentiousness, gently steering me to various critical texts he thought I should read. Some ten years later, that MA enabled John Holmes to secure for me a profoundly underpaid and overworked adjunct teaching job at Tufts, my first venture into academia.

That halcyon year in graduate school I had another mentor, Albert Guerard Jr., who had, along with Mark Shorer and Otto Schoen-René, team-taught English 1, a survey of English lit course I took as a freshman. Guerard conducted the most exciting graduate seminar of my brief academic career, a course John Simon, who went on to fame as a theater critic, was also enrolled in. I was high on Conrad, John on Gide, and all ten or twelve of us in the seminar were in Guerard's thrall, meeting ahead of time in the Hayes Bickford cafeteria to try out our literary theories and repairing there after class to continue the dialogue.

It didn't occur to me to take note of the total absence of women faculty at Harvard. How myopic I was to complete four years as an undergrad, a fifth in grad school blissfully unaware of their exclusion!

We had two babies in eighteen months and very little money. Most of our peers were in the same boat. The prevailing postwar temper cried out for stability, family, and a secure future. Most of us thought we wanted three, possibly four children, and we wanted to have them all close together so they could share their childhoods. We all read Dr. Spock religiously, who comforted us that we were probably doing things right without even knowing it.

Evenings and many weekends, Victor took over the child care as I researched various topics at the Boston Medical Library.

Gradually I became a rather successful ghost writer for a German psychiatrist whose sentences in English were impenetrable. I wrote papers for a surgeon doing experiments on burns, papers he then delivered at symposia as his own, and I ghosted for other physicians to whom my satisfied patrons referred me. Five dollars an hour was munificent pay. And while it wasn't exactly literary criticism, I was a freelance writer at last!

I don't think it occurred to us that we were in the vanguard in terms of marriage and parenting. Certainly it helped to be poor. We shared the household chores of laundry and marketing, folding diapers (we couldn't afford the then-burgeoning home diaper service and, besides, we got a lot of these essentials free from Victor's workplace), amusing toddlers and sitting up with them through chicken pox and earaches. We read aloud to them and to each other, took them to free concerts on the banks of the Charles River in Boston and on day trips in the country.

We both had felt shortchanged in our own childhoods; Victor's father had died, possibly a suicide, when Victor was five. His mother never quite got over her grief. She became a professional widow. And there were money problems during the ensuing Depression, problems that distracted her to the point where her youngsters received little more nurturing than food and shelter. Although I had grown up in a well-to-do household, my mother and I were at loggerheads. We could not please each other. She had, as she put it, "gone to the well four times" to get a daughter, but I was not the compliant female she had longed for. It was a cold relationship for my brothers as well. We kids were farmed out early, first to a nursemaid, then to day camps and overnight camps. I cannot remember a single family excursion other than the annual pilgrimage to Atlantic City to visit my father's mother. Victor and I were going to do a better job of parenting.

With three kids under the age of five, plus assorted household dogs and cats, every day was a challenge. The poetry never went away, however. I continued to write in the interstices of time between laundry and chauffeuring, between part-time medical editorial writing and part-time teaching of freshman composition at Tufts University. We bought a modest home in the suburbs. In 1963 we bought a derelict farm in New Hampshire.

Everyone grew up. The large children turned into interesting, even delightful, adults. We are still partners in possession of a long marriage, with too many horses, too ambitious a vegetable garden, too many sugar maples to tap. The family gathers in at Christmas and again in August. It's the way it should be, we think, and we are grateful for it.

Swimming and Writing

I can't remember when I learned to swim. I know that as a small child of four or five I was terrified of the waves at Atlantic City, where we spent a few weeks each summer in my grandmother's Victorian apartment overlooking the beach. Waves that seemed reasonable to adults toppled me even though I was held firmly by hand, perhaps even swung between two grown-ups who endeavored to lift me over the largest combers. That was when I learned the little ditty: "I hate to swallow ocean and it's all God's fault. He could have put in sugar but He went and put in salt."

The waves were so menacing some days that lifeguards strung ropes out to their rowboats and bathers were forbidden to go beyond the prescribed limit. Bathing in saltwater was thought to ensure good health. Weekend afternoons in July there would be hundreds of people of all ages and stages crowded into the roped-off areas, nervously policed by lifeguards continually manning their oars to hold their positions. Sometimes they put on exhibitions to demonstrate their skills to the general public. They swam short choppy crawl strokes with their heads held high, breasting out over the waves the way I imagined seals might do. I was in awe of these burly magnificent showmen and their noble calling.

Swallowing ocean makes you wary. This awareness of the nervous balance between staying alive and drowning taught me to respect the power and majesty of nature. However much I might have longed to be one, I learned early that I was not an amphibian.

And then one magical day, I floated with my face in the water. My feet rose to the surface of their own accord. I blew bubbles, exulting in my buoyancy. At a rather casually run day camp in Ambler, Pennsylvania, the summer I was eight, I turned into a swimmer. Released from the Tadpole Group into deep water, I learned how to execute the sidestroke. That same memorable summer I learned how to jump into deep water and graduated to performing a rudimentary dive.

Breaststroke, elementary backstroke, Australian crawl, and back crawl came later, at sleep-away camp in the Berkshires. Back crawl was done in the Eleanor Holm tradition, a sort of straight-armed windmill style. The butterfly stroke was harder to master. In those days, before the dolphin undulations were developed, it was accompanied by a whip kick. And the inverted breaststroke, my favorite resting stroke, taught me to accept wavelets washing over my face as I glided on my back.

Summer camp was my salvation. I returned year after year, first as camper, then junior counselor, then assistant to the head of the waterfront. I finally succeeded to the top post the summer after my sophomore year in college. That same year I studied English poetry from Chaucer to Robert Bridges and began to appreciate the rules of prosody, but there was no conscious overlap between my twin responsibilities. While poetry absorbed me in the winter, there was no question of my loyalties from June to Labor Day. Only marriage removed me – rescued me, my husband likes to say – from those hectic and happy Berkshire summers.

The waterfront counselor, my first three summers as an overnight camper, was a member of the Dartmouth swimming team and he possessed a real stopwatch. Nor did he discriminate between the genders; girls were encouraged to race against each other and against the boys from the other side of the campus as well. At ages eleven or twelve, we females took great pleasure in besting the skinny shivering preadolescent males we were ranged against.

In addition to his stopwatch, Johnny-the-Dartmouth-Man had an eight-millimeter movie camera. He took pictures of our crawl strokes, then played the film back for us slow-motion, critiquing our faults. It was wonderful to be taken seriously. What I learned about the freestyle, or Australian, crawl was how to achieve maximum thrust with minimum exertion. Many years later, I learned to apply the same criterion to the poem, seeking a seemingly artless effect with the maximum thrust – pages and pages of worksheets subjected to formal compression.

I remember practicing my racing dive those summer afternoons until my entire torso ached from the repetitive harsh contact with the lake's surface. I remember practicing the cross-chest carry, the surface dive to retrieve a ten-pound weight in ten feet of water. I remember wrinkled fingers and toes from long immersion and deep suntans, then the swimmer's badge of honor.

My idyllic summers at camp also included distance swimming and I think it was there, crossing the mile-wide lake solo (accompanied by a counselor in a rowboat), that I first began to match the rhythm of memorized poems to the stroke-breath-stroke of the trudgen crawl. I swam to A.E. Housman's cadences, his classic romantic elegiac voice suffusing my long-distance swims with gentle melancholy. "With rue my heart is laden," I droned, swiveling my head for the next intake of air. "For golden friends I had," I bubbled, breathing out into the water.

Summer camp was the setting for my poem "Morning Swim," which speaks to those early-morning solitary swims half a mile down the lake, half a mile back. It was my dearest dream at that time to become a member of the women's Olympic swim team and in pursuit of this goal – I hesitate to put the connection into words – I merged with the water, moving in and through this medium that recalled unconsciously the amniotic fluids where I had begun. "Morning Swim" concludes: "My bones drank water; water fell / through all my doors. I was the well // that fed the lake that met my sea / in which I sang 'Abide with Me.'" I hesitate to undercut these lines with further comment, but that they convey a sense of merging with what Conrad called "the destructive element" is obvious.

By now I had acquired my American Red Cross junior and senior lifesaving certificates as well as the advanced swimmer's logo, proudly if somewhat crookedly sewn to my best bathing suit, the one I wore for showing off at swim meets. Now I was swimming winters as well at the Broadmoor pool in downtown

Philadelphia, where I had the good fortune to encounter an exacting instructor. I wish I could remember Alex's last name but I can never forget his earnest manner, his insistence on exactitude. He inspired me to be even more economical of breath and stroke. Nothing was to be squandered, everything was to be streamlined to achieve perfect harmony with the water. "Now, class," Alex would intone, "I want you simultaneously, at the same time, together..." to perform whatever the next maneuver was to be. The parallel with poetry is obvious – economy of expression, nothing squandered – but even more delicious was his entirely innocent redundancy. *Simultaneously at the same time together* became a kind of mantra for me, something I muttered grittily to myself in the last turn of the 400-meter freestyle.

Just before my eighteenth birthday, the directors of the summer camp I had attended faithfully from age eleven, paid my tuition to attend a two-week-long crash course in Annapolis, Maryland. The goal was to acquire my Water Safety Instructor's certificate. Once I passed this course they intended to hire me back as a senior waterfront counselor. It was a watershed moment (no pun intended) for me; it provided entry into a possible career teaching swimming and lifesaving and training other swim instructors.

Teaching Junior Lifesaving to a group of shivering twelve-year-olds gave rise to one of my early poems, "Junior Lifesaving," which again addresses the paradox of immersion in and giving in to the water:

> Class, I say, this is
> the front head release.
> And Adam's boy, whose ribs
> dance to be numbered aloud,
> I choose to strangle me.
> Jaw down in his embrace
> I tell the breakaway.
> Now swimming in the air

we drown, wrenching the chin,
clawing the arm around.
...
Class, I say (and want
to say, children, my dears,
I too know how to be afraid),
I tell you what I know:
go down to save.

That same year I was approached by a representative of Billy Rose's Aquacade, an outfit that performed synchronized swimming routines in public pools and hotels around the country. Synchronized swimming was touted as poetry in motion. A perfect fit. The pay seemed munificent, $100 a week plus all expenses. A chaperon was provided; travel was by streamlined bus – in the forties, travel by air was uncommon and expensive. An adventure! My father was horrified and forbade me even to consider such an offer. He had never particularly approved of my swimming addiction in high school and found it offensive that I came to supper with my long hair only hastily toweled, still dripping chlorinated droplets onto the dinnerware. Even when I made the swim team at college he felt I was wasting time better spent in intellectual pursuits.

For the poet, nothing is ever all for nothing. This incident worked its way into a poem, "Life's Work," ostensibly about my mother, whose desire to be a concert pianist was thwarted by her stern, Germanic father. The poem describes my eighteen-year-old self at the dinner table, inwardly rebelling, outwardly conforming:

My mouth chewed but I was doing laps.
I entered the water like a knife.
I was all muscle and seven doors.
A frog on the turning board.
King of the Eels and the Eel's wife.

In each of these figures of speech, I am something other than human: first, as narrow, as precise (and perhaps dangerous) as a knife; then, a creature made all of muscle, with seven orifices; next, the magical amphibious frog, equally at home in and out of water; and finally, the royal and androgynous Eel and Wife of the Eel, wily, swift, and incredibly graceful in their element.

—⌘—

I longed to go to Wellesley College because it had a regulation-size swimming pool surrounded by high windows and an underwater observation room that permitted close analysis of the swimmer's movements. The admissions committee rejected me. Radcliffe was my second choice. Radcliffe, however, had only a dingy little swimming pool five yards shy of standard length and housed in a basement room without windows.

Team sports got only a cursory nod from the administration; back then, Cliffies were notorious for their indifference to athletic pursuits. Thus it was no great feat to make the team. Our only competitions were with nearby schools. Tufts's Jackson and Brown's Pembroke are two I remember. Of course neither Tufts nor Brown Universities were coeducational in the forties. Women's teams were condescended to, underfunded and unpublicized. Still, we took ourselves very seriously; we trained, we strategized, and frequently we lost. But the camaraderie of belonging to a team, the participatory democracy of choosing who was to swim what stroke in the medley, the cheerful determination to do the best we could with the personnel we had made my four undergraduate years in that dank basement a rich experience.

My poem "400-Meter Freestyle," the only "shaped" poem I have ever written (the beginnings and endings of each line reproduce the flip turn at the end of each lap), arose from my memory of those glory days of college competition, the somersaulting turns, the punishing pace. The poem is written in the male persona only because at the time of its composition – the late fifties – I did not think the average reader would be willing to invest much emotion in a female competitive swimmer. The language of the poem attempts to describe the event from two points of view, that of the swimmer and the viewpoint of the observer:

THE GUN full swing the swimmer catapults and cracks

                                                    s

                                                    i

                                                    x

feet away onto that perfect glass he catches at

...

...We watch him for signs. His arms are steady at

                                                    t

                                                    h

                                                    e

catch, his cadent feet tick in the stretch, they know

    t

  h

    e

lesson well. Lungs know, too; he does not list for

                                                    a

                                                    i

                                                    r...

When our children were young, I renewed my Water Safety Instructor's certificate and became head counselor of the waterfront at a Girl Scout day camp not far from our home in suburban Boston. It was a hectic schedule, getting three kids ready to catch the morning bus that transported us to the camp, monitoring more than a hundred youngsters all day in and out of the water, and experiencing a rising sense of helplessness as I was unable to teach our youngest child and only son, then going on six, how to swim. This was a child who almost died at birth and subsequently spent his first weeks on oxygen in an incubator.

"Poem for My Son" came out of that difficult beginning,

heightened for me by our son's inability to take to the water with the other kids of staff members at camp. I could point to at least half a dozen other early poems of mine that attend to the art of learning how to swim, learning to perform the simple sidestroke, as in "The Lesson": and let us change sides, remembering / it is the top leg goes forward / forming the blade of the scissors..." At the close of the lesson,

> I lie flat
> on the rib cage of a canoe
> assaulting the thin edge of water,
> holding the noon on my eyelids.
> Now there is only the water
> and the sound of water forming
> under the slope of my spine.

It seems I am once again attempting to pinpoint the relationship of human to water, water as friend but also as foe. The sensuous experience, the closeness of body to pond as the speaker of the poem lies sunbathing in a canoe, ends with three lines repeated from the body of the poem, followed by an ominous fourth:

> wherefore the season reverses,
> the dragonfly clicks and is gone,
> the cattails resist in the marshes,
> drowned men thrust under my bone.

I still swim regularly, from mid-June to mid-September in our own pond on the farm, and catch-as-catch-can the rest of the year when I'm on the road doing readings and residencies. Swimming competitively taught me the value of daily discipline, for muscles unused soon atrophy. Lines of poems unattended to, disappear. Rilke said it best when he counseled the young poet to "keep holy all that befalls." For me, swimming is another way of keeping holy.

Motherhood and Poetics

I came to motherhood in 1948 at the age of twenty-four. I came to poetry in desperation during my third pregnancy, through the back door.

Although I was an ardent adolescent poet, a trait I shared with virtually all the poets I know, I was shocked into abandoning creative writing my freshman year in college. My instructor, the late Wallace Stegner, who I now realize was only a few years older and wiser than I, had told me to "Say it with flowers but for God's sake don't write poems about it." An unworldly seventeen-year-old, I had been exempted from taking the standard freshman English composition class and thrust into an upper-level course in which I was the quivering naïf. Stegner was right; my poems were sentimental and morbid but, "when lonely on an August night I lie / wide-eyed beneath the mysteries of space," they were cries from the heart. After his scrawled comment I put them aside for several years.

Nineteen fifty-three was the winter of my discontent. Pregnant, restless, unhappy with my closet poems that seemed fixated on death and loss, I was overwhelmed with guilt that I was not happy. For didn't I have everything any modern woman could want? What was this nagging unease, and where would it lead?

In 1946, the summer that I graduated from college and married, I had been offered a fellowship to attend the University of Grenoble, repository of Stendhal's manuscripts. I declined easily, thoughtlessly, without regret. The war was over; we were recklessly in love and plunged headlong into our new lives. Marry in haste, goes the aphorism. It wasn't that I was repenting at leisure. But I was looking back hard at the road not taken.

A passage in Sonya Tolstoy's diary, written while Lev was absent on one of his many excursions, speaks to this situation. She had totally dedicated her life to caring for him and the many children they had together, "all of which," she said, "is happiness of a kind, but why do I feel so woeful all the time?" I had arrived at that place.

I couldn't admit that I was depressed. I began to write light verse, a genre I had always admired. I would have preferred to write librettos for Broadway musicals, but filler verse was at least within my grasp. A small poem is infinitely portable. The strictures of rhyme and meter could be sorted through in my head while doing the daily chores.

For $3.95 I bought a text by Richard Armour, *Writing Light Verse,* and slavishly followed his prescriptions. My card file was a little cedar box labeled "Recipes." On three-by-five cards I kept track of every poem I submitted and vowed a private vow that if I were still unpublished by the time this third baby arrived, I would abandon the entire enterprise.

In March, *The Christian Science Monitor* printed a four-liner I still remember:

> There never blows so red the rose
> so sound the round tomato
> as March's catalogs disclose
> and yearly I fall prey to.

Our son Danny was born three months later. By the end of the year I was publishing four- to eight-liners in journals as disparate as *The Saturday Evening Post, Baby Talk,* and *The New York Herald Tribune.* Heartened by my acceptances, I scribbled away at odd hours. The two older children were in nursery school; the new baby took lovely long naps. I adopted the slovenly practice of going directly to my desk whenever silence reigned and picked away at my bone pile of ideas while dishes and laundry, unmade beds and unvacuumed rooms yawned. I learned early that one can do housework and tend to minors at the same time, chauffeur an underage cellist to a lesson and occupy that quiet hour in the car with a worksheet. To this day, much of my best writing time takes place in what I think of as the interstices. The anonymity of a bustling airport between connections is one of my favorite workplaces.

In 1957, with three children under the age of ten, I screwed my courage to the sticking point and signed up for a poetry workshop conducted by poet and Tufts University professor John Holmes at The Boston Center for Adult Education. Anne Sexton and I met in that class.

I still carry Anne around with me, a vivid presence, a reminder of how humbly we began, first in John Holmes's workshop, then as members of the New England Poetry Club, which at that time was composed mostly of Boston Brahmins of a certain age.

Enter two outlanders, two young mothers from the suburbs, Anne in high heels, pancake makeup, and with flowers in her hair, I dressed as Anne has characterized me, "the frump of frumps." Because Holmes, the Club's president, had proposed us, we were admitted to the inner sanctum, but only, we were cautioned, on a provisional basis. Within six months we had each had a poem accepted by *The New Yorker* and another by *Harper's,* magazines the older members aspired to but rarely reached. Our provisional status was hastily dropped.

Our kids' ages overlapped only slightly. Anne's older daughter Linda and my youngest, Danny, were pretty much the same age, but Anne became a golden sort of godmother to my daughters. They looked up to her as someone far more worldly and stylish than their own mother. And when Linda began to write poetry of her own in high school, I became her mentor and mother figure.

Anne performed the same function for my daughter Judy, who went on to win the Untermyer Award at Harvard in her junior year. When Anne formed her chamber-rock group, Anne Sexton and Her Kind, Danny composed the musical background to her recitation of "The Little Peasant" (from *Transformations*). It has been singled out for its wit and jauntiness.

Back in the late fifties, leaving our little children in the care of husbands or baby-sitters, Anne and I trudged off together to poetry readings all over Greater Boston. Some were electrifying – Robert Frost playacting the part of lovable old curmudgeon, unforgettable John Crowe Ransom, a pink, bald Kewpie doll of a man rocking onto his toes while reciting "She in terror fled from the marriage chamber" (From "Two in August") in a cadence that echoes still in my head. We observed, rather than heard, Marianne Moore's reading at Wellesley – she was all but inaudible.

We were inching our way into the inner sanctum by way of publications and readings. We were striking out like Conrad's secret sharer, stroking into the deep waters of an ocean that had until then virtually excluded women from the swim. That we had young children at home was a fact we rarely alluded to. Children were an encumbrance, domestic duties held a woman back. We both knew this.

Getting published at all was a triumph. Everyone knew that men wrote the really interesting poems about war, politics, hunting: in short, poems about the world. Women only wrote about relationships, emotions, domestic arcana. Poetry by women was soupy and romantic. It was immature. No wonder women poets frequently hid behind their first-name initials. We wrote in dread of being labeled little three-name Letitia ladies.

For two aspiring female poets, a leap of the Grand Canyon was no more formidable than daring to establish a profoundly secure friendship. It was a bond I had initially resisted, having only the year before lost a good friend to suicide during a postpartum depression – Anne's first hospitalization, after the birth of her second child, had been for a postpartum depression. (Doesn't this say something about the culture, the medical establishment, women's roles in the United States of the fifties?) This bond gradually tightened until I understood I had finally found the one best friend and confidante my teenage years had never provided.

Over the last thirty years I have acquired several true-blue women friends and confidantes, poets and writers in other genres, but it seems I had to traverse some rocky terrain before I could reach out to others of my sex. Part of this resistance was cultural. I grew up understanding that a man's world was in every way superior to a woman's. At cocktail and dinner parties, on one side of the room men conducted in-depth conversations about politics, religion, baseball. On the other, women talked about sterilizing infant formulas, how to prepare carrot sticks, where to find replacements for broken china patterns. Intelligent, well-educated women demeaned themselves in this way.

The change was gradual but the truth is that the women's movement, which sanctioned assertiveness and creativity, changed my life and the lives of my contemporaries. For some of us the change was subtle, a filtering down of new beliefs. For others it meant royal warfare, divorces, new destiny. Certainly knowing and loving Anne helped me to know and love women, appreciate my own gender, see ever more clearly the struggle in which we were engaged to make our own way, to legitimize our own goals and ideals.

After our successful foray into the Boston Center's poetry workshop, five of us: Holmes, George Starbuck, Sam Albert, Sexton, and I, developed a workshop of our own. For more than two years we met every other week in one another's houses and wrangled long into the night over poems in process. My children, seeing me set out glasses and plates, would ask, "Company? Who's coming?" "No," I'd say. "It's just the workshop." They would set up a collective groan. "Oh, not the poets again! Can we go sleep in the room over the garage?"

I don't know how Anne and I managed not to intrude on each other's voice. We listened, sympathized, made suggestions. But we were operating under very different influences. And from the very beginning of exploring each other's worksheets we both knew intuitively that it was essential to preserve our individuality. The mutual influence led of course to some cross-fertilization. I was able to become more personal, more daring in my poems. Anne perhaps took from me the advice that constraints of meter and form are paradoxically freeing agents.

Of course we had no women mentors. Although between us we knew a dozen of Millay's sonnets by heart, although we admired Marianne Moore from afar and were hugely in awe of Elizabeth Bishop, our poet models were all male. Sexton drew heavily on Snodgrass and Lowell; I frankly studied and imitated Auden and Karl Shapiro.

At the tail end of the fifties I began to teach at Tufts University. Admittedly, it was only as an adjunct. As a part-time female, I was deemed eligible to teach freshman composition only to the physical-education majors and the dental technicians. My husband was genuinely pleased for me; even this low-paying job was a coup for a woman. We both understood the value of extra money coming in. Now that our third child was in kindergarten, I was able to arrange with a kind neighbor to pick him up and deliver him to the local grammar school three times a week when I commuted to Medford to meet my freshman composition classes.

Some of my neighbors were appalled that I would abandon my children in this wanton fashion. Others were not surprised, for by then they had stumbled upon my light verse in *Ladies' Home Journal* and *Good Housekeeping,* magazines they treasured. But it was clear to all that I was not sufficiently focused on my homemaker duties. These devoted mothers were hand-decorating birthday cakes, hand-sewing Halloween costumes, polishing their silver flatware, tending their backyard flower gardens, finding wholesome domestic outlets for their creative abilities.

Looking back, it is hard to believe how judgmental and corrosive these criticisms were to me. A little guilt makes the world go round, but I was almost convinced that I was shortchanging my children, a bad mother daring to nibble around the edges of an actual career.

In 1961, Sexton and I were both selected for charter membership in The Radcliffe Institute for Independent Study, later renamed The Bunting Institute. We were lionized, interviewed by the press and scrutinized by the local community. The Institute conferred legitimacy on our activities. I especially remember Anne saying that she had not previously been able to cut short a telephone conversation by saying that she was writing a poem; she would dissemble and announce that she was in the middle of making gravy, or had a cake in the oven. (Gorgeous lies. A cook she was not.)

Election to the Institute meant social intercourse with gifted women in other fields. Sculptors, painters, historians, scientists, all came together for the weekly seminars. Among us we counted at least two dozen small children. We were sharing the same space and the same struggle and we talked about it freely. A lot of flatware went blessedly unpolished.

Coincidentally in 1960 I published my first children's book, a story in rhyme called *Sebastian and the Dragon*. Inspired by my children, who were enthusiastic listeners, I wrote four more books the following year; in all, I wrote and published twenty juveniles. Initially, I viewed my success in this genre as an embarrassment. Kiddie-lit was not something a serious self-respecting poet ought to undertake. It simply reinforced the domestic-poet stereotype. It was a given that the distinctly female voice, as well as the voice directed to children, represented inferior art. But several well-known male poets – William Jay Smith, Ted Hughes, Randall Jarrell, John Ciardi – were also invading the genre, conferring aesthetic validation upon it.

During the sixties, Sexton and I wrote four children's books together. I confess that our approach was downright giddy. We took turns at the typewriter and at dictating the story line. Whoever was typing at the moment had veto power. On at least one occasion we took turns floating around in Anne's swimming pool and worked with the typewriter precariously balanced on the lip. For years after, we argued over who had come up with the critical line that provides the fulcrum to *Joey and the Birthday Present* (Joey is a white mouse): "And they both agreed that a birthday present could not run away."

Now we were heroes to our kids. We were writing books they could be proud of, take to school, read aloud to youngsters in classes below theirs. And what a good time we'd had!

I've since written, but have not been able to publish, three children's stories that were inspired by my grandchildren. I see an extra jaunty note creeping into my poetry, too. But looking back I understand my reticence about the juvenile books and the light verse. Although several very successful light versifiers were male – Shel Silverstein, Ogden Nash – light verse bore the taint of domesticity. Who today reads Phyllis McGinley, a superb poet? I have many of her poems by heart, particularly "Ballade of Lost Objects," which is chiseled on my brain pan. Think of finding four good rhymes for her refrain line, *"Where in the world did the children vanish?"* McGinley makes it look easy. Here are her daughters:

> rending the air with
> Gossip and terrible radios.
> Neither my friends nor quite my foes,
> Alien, beautiful, stern, and clannish,
> Here they dwell, while the wonder grows:
> Where in the world did the children vanish?

Anyone with daughters will resonate with those lines.

There is still a bountiful supply of sexist condescension that regards poems about domestic relationships as possibly charming and appealing but unworthy of serious critique. Poems about women's bodies and women's bodily functions still arouse a degree of terror and antipathy in certain quarters, but when I look back forty years to the seminal poems of Sexton, Kizer, Plath, and other innovators, I am heartened.

I have shamelessly drawn on the lives of my children as a sourcebook for my work. The intimate familial relationships, particularly mother-daughter ones, fed my poetry. The serious artistic voice has no gender, in my opinion, but it may assuredly take a stance. From the earliest observations of separation ("Nightmare" and "Poem for My Son," from *Halfway*), to the anguish as grown offspring leave home ("Address to the Angels," "Making the Jam without You," "The Journey," "For My Son on the Highways of His Mind," "Sunbathing on a Rooftop in Berkeley," "Seeing the Bones," from *Selected Poems, 1960–1990*), to somewhat more distanced and nuanced poems like "The Bangkok Gong" (*Selected Poems*), "After the Cleansing of Bosnia" (*Connecting the Dots*), my poems have been inextricably enmeshed in my role as mother.

This role has informed almost every poem I have written. Indeed, even as I have turned more of my attention to the natural world of farm and forest, especially to the nonverbal communication that takes place between humans and other creatures, I would have to acknowledge that the animals, my confederates, constitute our second family. With children grown and gone, we continue to raise and care for horses, dogs, cats, and in summer, a friend's visiting ewes.

Even with these commitments, I am not able, it seems, to eschew writing about grandchildren: vide "A Game of Monopoly in Chavannes," and "We Stood There Singing" (*Selected Poems*), and "The Height of the Season," "Beans Beans Beans," and "The Riddle of Noah" (*Connecting the Dots*). Yet I do edit and self-censor my work to keep from crossing certain boundaries of privacy and decorum. I am fond of saying to fearful students who turn in poems about family members, "Now that you have made art of it, it belongs to the ages." But of course there are matters of taste and tact. Sometimes just putting a searing poem away for a few days, months, or years will solve the problem. Sometimes, as you "await the birth-hour of a new clarity," as Rilke advised Mr. Kappus, a path around the emotional obstacle will appear. And eventually, truly, it will belong to the ages.

October 4, 1995

I am sitting on the terrace in full sun today, October 4, the twenty-first anniversary of Anne's suicide, paying my own kind of homage to that event. On my lap, Peter Davison's *The Fading Smile,* his account of the poetic happenings of 1955 to '60 in and around Boston. In my head, some lines from Virginia Woolf's diaries which she kept for nearly thirty years, writing in them "at a rapid haphazard gallop," allotting to them a half hour a day at late afternoon tea. "Unpraised, I find it hard to start writing in the morning," Virginia Woolf noted. When I first came to that word, I misread it as "upraised." My best writing time is morning. I often wake in a flood of memories, old sensations, sometimes with Anne's face, its slight but decisive asymmetry accentuated by her astonishingly piercing blue eyes, or with her gesticulating arms vivaciously forcing home a point, the whole scene wreathed in cigarette smoke.

It's hard for me to come to terms with the fact that I'm history, cited in texts such as Peter's, that our friendship burgeoned from two suburban housewives workshopping their poems over the telephone in between the homely tasks of laundry and chauffeuring of children, to figures of considerable stature in contemporary American poetry. I find myself referred to as having helped revise social expectations of poets and even of poetry, and of having effected this change by writing out of a previously inadmissible constellation of feelings. The shock of recognition we were taught to expect from poetry, the "frisson" that comes from my poetry is new, different, distinctively female, say some reviewers. I am still startled by being told that I was in the forefront of these changes.

Certainly, had Anne lived, she would have won these and far greater accolades, for she dared to break new ground and old taboos from the very beginning. Much of my own courage in confronting the swamp of childhood, the shifting miasma of maternal and erotic feelings arose out of our poetic sisterhood.

Even though all of us close to Anne knew we would lose her eventually, that she would somehow die by her own hand after innumerable rehearsals, I was bowled over by her suicide. Shocked, grieved, outraged, terribly angry at her deception, for hadn't she just said quite cheerfully, "See you tomorrow?" – all that gamut of emotions the psychiatrists have cataloged into stages, the ladder we must climb to the top labeled Coming to Terms. So when the media descended clamoring for interviews, I didn't cope very well. I didn't want to talk to *The New York Times* or *The Boston Globe*. It was excruciatingly painful for me to deliver that little address at the memorial service in Boston University's Marsh Chapel, even though John Cheever's kind presence helped sustain me. I remember *Mirabella* magazine offered me $3,000 – a sizable payment back then – to do an article on our friendship. I replied that I would not, could not, use our relationship for personal gain. I desperately did not want the notoriety that attached to Annie's death. I wanted her back, quite simply! I wanted to save alive the warmth we had provided for each other, not make book on it.

During our early friendship we were both members of the New England Poetry Club. For a long time, it seemed some of the members had trouble sorting us out. We were both tall and slender. We were young. We both had dark hair. But Anne was flamboyant and outspoken, nervous yet brash; I played the rational, almost withdrawn, intellectual. Anne said, "You know why they can't tell us apart? They can't figure out who's the Jew and who's the kook."

Anne's career took off like a rocket. Mine escalated gradually, but we were both gaining recognition in national publications. We were each invited to give readings from time to time and we each suffered terrible anxiety over these performances. Annie dissolved her fears in alcohol. I too downed a couple of martinis beforehand whenever feasible and although it helped a little, I was still subject to panic attacks while I was locked up in delivering a poem. It took me years to overcome this terror, even after I understood it intellectually.

Somewhere out in the audience lurked the Thirteenth Fairy, a mother surrogate who was watching me critically, and whom I had to best, rise above, in order to succeed. And that was the dilemma, wanting to succeed but not daring symbolically to sacrifice the mother to do so. My father used to quote these lines from his boyhood memorizations: "I'm sorry that I spelled that word. I hate to rise above you / because (the low voice lower still) because, you see, I love you."

One of my ploys was to choose very short poems to begin with, for when the panic struck, I could talk my way around it if I was not held prisoner by the exact words on the page. I prayed to have enough breath to push out the words before the demon of hyperventilation claimed me. Later, I learned how to structure a reading by choosing an opening poem or two that elicited audience response – laughter, applause – thereby setting the stage for my gradual shift into more personal or more formally demanding poems.

Our friendship began over poems. It seemed logical that it would continue back home in our suburban lives. Early on, though, we discovered that this was not to be a couples' friendship. Victor and Kayo had little or nothing in common. They went skiing together once, as I recall, and managed to spend a day on the mountain without riding the chairlift side by side more than once. They were cordial but distant with each other. I don't know if they actually disliked each other, or if Anne's and my intense friendship served as a constraint.

On the poetry scene of the fifties, Anne and I were on hand to assist in picking up and delivering back to the airport many a male poet visitor. We were suitably flattered when told "You drive like a man" as one or the other of us made a heroic dash through traffic to get the poet to his plane on time. Told "You write like a man," we took it for the supreme compliment that it was. I don't know the source of the saying "There was a man so poor he fell in love with jail," but it exactly fit our situation.

Merely getting published was an occasion for rejoicing. I remember John Ciardi's candor on the subject. John became a kind of mentor to me at Bread Loaf some years later; then poetry editor of *The Saturday Review of Literature,* he said, "I'd love to publish one of the poems in this batch, but I published a woman last month." This struck me as entirely reasonable ("a man so poor...").

I remember that Anne and I went to Manhattan with John Holmes, though the occasion – possibly to hear him read at The Poetry Society of America – escapes me. He took us to meet Bob Silvers, poetry editor of *Harper's.* To be shepherded through the streets of lower Manhattan by this distinguished poet and professor, to be ushered into the private office of the editor of a major publication thanks to Holmes's connection was impressive indeed. Was this really happening to the pawnbroker's daughter from Philadelphia and the daughter of the waste-wool merchant from Wellesley?

John's death from cancer in 1962 brought our workshop to a close. George had left the preceding year; Ted and Renée Weiss were in town for one semester while Ted taught at Brandeis, and we continued to meet through that term. Ted is a great punster and wit as well as an elegant wordsmith and he provided a necessary leavening.

For the storm cloud of John's disapproval of Anne's confessional voice weighed on all of us, but especially on me. He counseled me frequently not to become involved with her. There were the letters that came the morning after workshop; in those days, mail was delivered overnight and two mail deliveries a day pretty much guaranteed that a missive written at white heat and mailed at midnight would reach the addressee before two PM the next day. John felt that Anne would destroy me even as she would destroy herself. (He had considerable insight here, as his first wife had committed suicide. It was rumored that she did so by slitting her wrists in his study and some read this as an act of vengeance against his passion for poetry.) Since Holmes was my Christian academic daddy, since he had gotten me my first bona fide academic appointment, had shoehorned me into the Poetry Society of America, where I promptly won one of their annual awards, had cosseted me and invited me to meet the major poets of the day as they passed through Boston, I found it excruciating to defy him. And yet, my own instincts told me that Sexton's early poems were brilliant, that they needed to be written, that she was blazing a trail for women to follow.

But beyond that. How to describe the welcome tentacles of our relationship? We were sisters, we were more than sisters. I, who had never had a sister, perhaps fantasized Anne as my own lately arrived true one. Anne, who had two blood sisters and felt little or no rapport with either of them, found in me the accepting model sibling she had fantasized.

We were both the youngest in our families and the youngest invariably perceives the world around her in a way very different from the older, hence wiser sibs. There is a struggle to be recognized, to be seen as worthy. We were able to cheer each other on, applaud every publication of a poem in a chain of magazines up from Richard Ashman's *New Orleans Poetry Review* to Howard Moss's selections for *The New Yorker*. I can't say I was never jealous of her stellar rise to fame. But if becoming a contract writer for *The New Yorker* couldn't happen to me, I reasoned, having it happen to Annie was the next best outcome.

Workshopping poems in process over the phone helped to train our ears. From this experience, I learned the value of having students read their work aloud in seminars, and by extension I came to appreciate all over again the intrinsic worth of having poems by heart. Later, face-to-face, going over poems we had heard in first draft, we learned how vital the shape of the poem is, the weight and look of the line itself. We hammered stuck pieces into form rather than abandon them. We preserved the raw works that refused to cohere and counseled each other to be patient, a bit of advice I have used effectively as a teacher. There are poems of Anne's that I rescued; I literally fished the first draft of "Cripples and Other Stories" out of her wastebasket. There are Sexton rearrangements in my own poems I can point to: the order of the final equivalents, "the mother bed, the ripe taste / of carrion, the green kiss" in "The Hermit Meets the Skunk," and in "The Presence," the tennis racket the porcupine is carrying was purely hers.

Anne's mental state, fragile at best, rose and fell like a fever chart. She had been variously diagnosed as depressed, as schizoid with depressive tendencies, even as schizophrenic, by a succession of psychiatrists. Except for the first one, Martin Orne, who rescued her out of the mental hospital and encouraged her to start writing, it seemed to me that she had a succession of disastrous shrinks. Orne later was pilloried by the American Psychiatric Association; the Pennsylvania Association wanted to defrock him because he had released to her biographer the confidential tapes Anne had made of their therapy sessions. The fact that several of these tapes were already in biographer Diane Wood Middlebrook's possession as part of the literary estate did not deflect the spoilers from their course.

I have never been able in my own mind to sort out the truths from the half-truths in this issue; the love affair her second psychiatrist conducted with her over a two-year period – sessions for which he was paid – earned this shrink not even a reprimand. And psychiatrist number three, who permitted Sexton to go off her medication and soon thereafter resigned from the case without finding her a suitable substitute, seems the most reprehensible of all.

To be caught up in this maelstrom of feeling, of diagnoses, hospitalizations, returns to the family, flights back to the hospital, and so on was exhausting. It was terribly hard on Anne's daughters and it taxed many of her friendships to the point of rupture. Volatile as she was, she was famous; new friends arrived as old ones decamped. Lovers, too, came and went. Anne found solitude intolerable and would do anything – anything! to fill the void with other human beings.

The marriage followed the course of a fever chart; Kayo found her depressions and hospitalizations intolerable. It was he who took up the slack, doing the marketing, cooking the meals, tending to the children's needs. But whenever Anne slipped away from him as she approached the edge of insanity, his anger erupted. In large part, though, he kept her sane by the sheer force of his will. Thorazine was the other stabilizing factor; when she took the medication, Anne's demon voices receded and indeed fell silent. But it made her sun-sensitive; it made her, she said, "woolly"; she could not write on Thorazine.

After the fact, I feel Anne had a right to her death. The knowledge that she had lost her poetic voice was the coup de grâce. Without her Muse, Sexton's life was meaningless and she left it. Looking back now, how ardently I wish we had been forced to resort to letters. If only those hours of phone calls – what Anne called "the hot ear" – workshopping poems, gossiping, confiding every intimate detail could be accessed on paper... and then what would we have? The double image of two narcissists, I say cynically.

Self-absorption, yes, but the subjective record of a friendship between two women writers who came fully to trust each other. We never lied to salve feelings. Had I been less forthright about those last several bad poems, would she have survived? I doubt it. Alcoholism and a seemingly unending supply of sleeping pills (a mystery, those pills: where did they come from?) cushioned the final descent. All of us saw the suicide coming but none of us was able to prevent it.

After the penultimate attempt on her life from which she had been rushed to the hospital to have her stomach pumped, furious with me, she had taxed me for intervening. Stung, I said then that as long as she was going to telegraph what she was planning, I would have to try to save her. (She had dialed her favorite priest and asked him to administer the last rites over the phone.)

Tears in her eyes, she said, "I promise you next time you won't know. No one will know."

And she kept her word. Our final lunch together in the break-fast room of our old house in Newton – half a tuna fish sandwich and two double vodkas for Anne – she seemed much calmer. Not happy, but content. We looked at the worksheets of a poem she had begun and we both agreed it had only a few redeeming qual-ities. She would rethink it, begin again. "Sometimes I think I'm just writing the same poem over and over," she said. I reminded her how fresh and wild the poems in *Transformations* were, how much of that rich material was still accessible. Not just Andersen and Grimm but the African folktales she had recently unearthed. A little rueful, she agreed. I walked out to her car with her. We hugged and parted. Four hours later, she was dead.

Sometimes we used to talk about sharing our old age, strolling along Fifth Avenue in space shoes individually crafted for our long, narrow feet. In this fantasy our handsome Dalma-tians trotted beside us. The vanity of high heels! My feet hurt still, just remembering.

I copied these lines from Carolyn Kizer:

> Forget the revolution they created
> with their raw confessional poetry;
> it's the suicides of two women
> which fascinate,
> not their way of working
> but their way of death.

The other poet, of course, is Sylvia Plath. Forget their way of death, I say, and focus on the poetry.

FOR ANNE AT PASSOVER

Cold Easter week and the hard buds, forming, shake
their miter caps at me. The tower bells
sing Christly sweet, and everywhere
new scents – honey and blood – work the air.

My students, outside the college halls, regroup,
share notes, and smoke. Coats open; no hats, no gloves.
Some metabolic principle
keeps them warm enough until the bell.
Or love. Or thoughts of going home. Time now,
we mind the syllabus which juxtaposes
Socrates, inviting the poison cup,
saying, *there is no fear that it will stop*
with me, and Jesus, apportioning His week,
however accidentally, with our Greek.

A kind of water-walking, Socrates
goes barefoot and uncaring over ice,
stands tranced through two dawns, is able
to drink all comers underneath the table,
and takes no lover in his night
except philosophy, *that dear delight.*

In air heavy as damask roses we read
the prison scene together. The weather abets us
and a great pocking rain commences.
We smell resurgence prickling our senses;

Son and sage hear voices. They keep no books,
but loose disciples on the world to tell

their missions, miracles, and choices;
in Christ's name, Joan burns for her voices.
In Christ's name shunned, historic news,
the Jews their owned stoned Jew refuse.

And Socrates, messiah true or false,
how might the Christ have come to take our sin
without you, *terribly at ease in Zion?*
You die now, for no man, and in no pain,
bathed and bedded according to the fashion,
friends who see you out your only Passion;
no nails, excepting as the soul is hung
against the flesh till death unfasten it.
One student says you sinned the sin of pride.
Another consecrates your suicide.

I say myths knit the world up when men die
for love; and if they lie, love needs the lie.
Time now. In Holy Week the tower bell
returns us to a faithful Friday rain.
Baggage and books, my students move about,
wish me a happy Easter, and go out.

II

Home by subway, I dare to see
my eye stare in my eye
and black it out;
and see my head, which best of all
I thought I knew,
elongate, squash, or disengage
itself; swim off and leave
my motiveless shoulders
lost in doubt.

66

Still, I get out
uptown, as decorous as the next,
feel useful in the buildings
out of habit,
peer through a window
at fat chocolate rabbits
and price Madonna lilies,
and buy an egg
with a crystal candy scene
sweetly inside – a peephole
for the eye of a child –
and look before I eat,
and put up my umbrella
in the three o'clock street.

They have unpinned Him in the rain.
Cabs spin from St. Philip's
and cars unpark
and I walk where disbelief
clacks at my soul,
an old god in my pocket
worrying the hole;
now all the saving bells begin.
I could not make Him to unmake my sin.

III

Tonight, the damask cloth laid, the loving cup
brimmed with sweet wine, I think of those my kin
who sat that Friday, inviting Elijah in
and swore he never came, nor comes again.
I think of Judas, the prophecy fetched up
to truth at our mutual season: yours to take
your pierced and honored Son out of His cave
and sing *resurgam,* drink His winy life;
       there at the rail for pity's sake

redeem yourself, all men, as if
there were still time in this hard-budding time;

and mine to mind another book: remind
my blood relations we are marked in the blood
of an earlier lamb, and call God good,
Who thumped our Moses so to send us out
and turned aside and hardened Pharaoh's heart
        ten times, Antagonist! to put
    us on that dusty pathway through
Your hot sea. So we come to praise You.

Yearly, the youngest child, asking why
this night is different from all other nights,
is told, his soft mouth crammed with bittersweet,
the bondage years in Egypt, and in some way
learns to perpetuate them from that day.
I remember my father's mother boiled
chickens with their feet on, and we ate,
blasphemous modern children, from her plate
both meat and milk and stayed up loved and late,
no letter law applying to a child.
I have sealed her in me, her fierce love
        of kindred all she had to give,
        and my drowned Polish ancestry,
washed out of Europe, rises up in me.

We pray tonight, dip herbs, and pour out wine,
forever what we are. I hear the rain
swelling the hard buds, all our fetishes
the simple sum of promises or wishes:
a radioactive rain in Pakistan
and Haifa, Yucca Flats, the Vatican,
        on all my kind: Manhattan rich

or Yemen poor, who break hard bread
tonight and bless their unforgotten dead.

What do we do, who eat to celebrate
with Eucharist and matzoh man's old fate?
I take a funny comfort, reading how
Bakongo folk, hard on the pulsing spew
of the afterbirth, would kiss that cord
and fix it in the belly of their god
       so that its navel bud protrudes
       where we are, mewling, swathed to hold
our secret in. We die, that knob unscaled.

       Now God forgive us where we live
       the ways we love are relative.
       Yours, Anne, the sacramental arts
       which divide Him in three parts;
       mine, the vengeful King of pride
       despite Whose arm His chosen died;
       theirs, the unction and the fuss
       who bless the lost umbilicus.

Guests of our glands, slaves to our origins,
we pray and eat tonight in greening weather.
Time swells the buds. A sharper rain begins;
we are all babes who suck at love together.

For Anne at Passover

When I opened a long-shelved copy of my first book, *Halfway* (Holt, Rinehart & Winston, 1961), a yellowed newspaper review fluttered from it. I suspect it was sent to me by some member of my Philadelphia family, possibly clipped from the *Philadelphia Inquirer,* but the sender failed to include any attribution. Today, I have no idea who wrote these lines:

> Mrs. Kumin has no bohemian vices or minority scars. Her 'Jewish heritage' mentioned in the blurb is not that of the slums nor even of the big city but is a biographical detail coupled with her love of the turbulent New England coast... One might wonder why the Jewish fact was brought up at all; it does not affect her rhetoric and enters her subject matter only through such *New Yorker*-ish exotica as 'our lop-eared Menorah... the membrane scrolls of Torah' in a poem of friendship to a Chinese... Her poem to Passover, the major statement in the collection, is equally a poem to Easter and to a rite of the Bakonga, the blended style perfectly mirroring a blended humanity.

Not only is my Jewishness a mere biographical detail for this reviewer; it is an exotic mannerism in the style of *The New Yorker,* a magazine to which I confess I aspired but in which I had at that time published only one poem, a secular paean to springtime.

I am not much given to quarrels with reviewers. It is bad form to protest any but the most egregious comment, and this one is raised, as it were, from the dead. Nevertheless, it seems to me that my Jewish consciousness is present in a goodly number of my poems from that first book onward. Frequently, my awareness is set against a Christian landscape, often Catholic, sometimes Southern Baptist.

I grew up in suburban Philadelphia, in an observant Reform Jewish household next door to the convent of the Sisters of St. Joseph, a teaching order, with whom we enjoyed cordial relations. For the sake of convenience – public school was a mile away – my parents enrolled me in their kindergarten. I further attended the first two years of elementary school in that cozy setting. But after I stole a rosary in my zeal to belong to the group (cf. "Mother Rosarine": "Wrong, born wrong for the convent games / I hunched on the sidelines beggar fashion"), my parents saw the light and hastily enrolled me in public school.

Thematically, the solidarity of the convent and the benevolence of Jesus present themselves in such poems as "Sisyphus" ("One day I said I was a Jew. / I wished I had. I wanted to."); "Mother Rosarine," which retells the theft of the praying beads; "Young Nun at Bread Loaf," which contrasts "Sister / Sister Elizabeth Michael / says we are doing Christ's work, we two. / She, the rosy girl in a Renoir painting" with my own agnosticism, "I, an old Jew"; "The Nuns of Childhood: Two Views," which narrates my adoring worship of the sisters in their habits. ("I, at age four with my darling nuns / ...am offered to Jesus, the Jewish child- / next-door....") Interested readers can follow the thread of my self-declared Jewish heritage through a spectrum of other poems ranging from "On Being Asked to Write a Poem on the Centenary of the Civil War" to "Living Alone with Jesus" ("Can it be I am the only Jew residing in Danville, Kentucky, / looking for matzoh in the Safeway and the A & P?"), "In the Absence of Bliss" ("The roasting alive of rabbis / in the ardor of the Crusades..."), "The Poet Visits Egypt and Israel," "The Riddle of Noah," and so on.

"For Anne at Passover" is the first poem in which I addressed the issue of living as a Jew in a Christian world. My friendship with Anne Sexton served as catalyst. We were by then – 1957 or

'58 – exchanging worksheets and ideas, arriving at the sisterhood that was to sustain us for the seventeen years of our friendship, which ended so abruptly with her suicide in 1974.

Given the vagaries of the calendar, Good Friday sometimes coincides with the first night of Passover, as I believe it did the year I was working on the poem. Despite my early Catholic education, I think I was a college student before I understood that *The Last Supper* depicted Jesus and his disciples ranged around the Seder table. It was not a point discussed in Sunday school classes at Rodeph Shalom, nor was it addressed in Fine Arts v, when we studied the composition of the painting, any more than the enthusiastic slaughter of Jews during the Crusades was a topic for investigation in History 1. Certainly I was a college freshman before I read the New Testament and encountered the aphoristic magic of The Sermon on the Mount. Moreover, I had never attended a church service (discounting my early indoctrination) until I was in my twenties.

I deplore the parochialism that still locks away recognition of the common heritage and religious practice between Jews and Christians and among Jews, Christians, and Muslims. To Anne at that time, Judaism was a curiosity, faintly tinged with disrepute. In her role of suburban housewife and mother, she was not much of a churchgoer. Nominally an Episcopalian, Easter signified new dresses and hats for her daughters and herself, Easter baskets, and Easter-egg hunts. The Hours of the Cross on Good Friday passed unacknowledged; the Resurrection appeared to have little resonance. Only years later as she undertook a spiritual quest for relevance and meaning in her personal life, an absolutism to cling to, did the intensely moving poems about Jesus and God the Father begin to take shape.

What Sexton knew about Jews was stereotypical anti-Semitic doctrine, acquired from the culture in which she was raised. The country club to which her parents belonged did not admit Jews. Jews were a token and somehow alien presence in the schools she attended. It was remarkable luck that we were able to break through all the barriers of prejudice and received opinions on both sides (on meeting her, my mother asked me in private, "Don't you have any good *Jewish* friends?"), and forge a deep personal and professional friendship.

Plato was part of the core curriculum in the freshman English class I taught at Tufts University. The readings were designed to encourage students to think through their philosophical and religious convictions, minimal as these were; the syllabus required me to read closely texts with which I had bare acquaintance from my own educational experience, and to stay one step ahead of the freshmen.

All of us young instructors were required to stick to the reading list, to hold common hour exams at midterm, to participate in composing multiple-choice questions for these exams, and to grade lengthy essay questions on the final. It was hard work and I am happy to reflect back on its rigors. *The unexamined life is not worth living,* the philosopher taught us. Without the noble example of Socrates, without the many-times-told tale of the New Testament and its central tragedy, without the Jewish notion of divine election from which derives the much-abused epithet, *the chosen people,* my life would have been, if not unexamined, at least underexamined.

Sexton and I were both formalists, loving the challenge of working in meter and rhyme and finding in the rigidity of a chosen form the permission to tackle emotionally charged or difficult topics. In this case, I more or less invented a nonce form as I went along and then tried to hew to it. In Part 1, I relied heavily on couplet rhymes to hold the stanzas together, balancing these against unrhymed lines that precede the rhymed ones. The poem opens with a stanza of 4 lines, followed by 10, then 6; then it repeats the pattern of 4, 6, 10, followed by a 6-liner.

The chronology is simple. During the final class before Easter recess, students discuss their reading assignment, the scene in which Socrates calmly drinks the cup of poison hemlock. It is an execution that invites sharp contrast with the crucifixion of Jesus; the Greek philosopher is "bathed and bedded according to the fashion, / friends who see you out your only Passion…"

Part II simply moves the narrator from the university to the city. It is three o'clock: "They have unpinned Him in the rain." I contrast the commercial aspect of Easter – store-window chocolate rabbits, eggs – with the church bells that announce the end of the Hours of the Cross. Even so, "I walk where disbelief / clacks at my soul, / an old god in my pocket / worrying the hole…" Here, the lines are looser, the rhymes present but irregular.

As deeply affecting as the crucifixion is, as deeply embedded in my consciousness from my early childhood experience in the convent, I continue to disbelieve in anything supernatural. As Santayana said, "Poetry is religion which is no longer believed." The god of any creed is for me little more than a metaphor; the resurrection of Jesus is perhaps the most elaborate and compelling metaphor of all.

Part III takes up the story of Passover. Judaism is to a pleasing and considerable extent a kitchen religion, perhaps reflecting its enclosure over centuries in the home or community. Every holiday seems to have its special foods. The Seder meal is long and full of ritual, with symbolic structures: the lamb shank, the roasted eggs, the bitter herb. The readings from the Haggadah are intended to recreate the exodus from Egypt for every child present. In a sense, the Seder service provides an indoctrination not dissimilar from, say, the Baltimore catechism, for every culture initiates its children into its own history. The roots of Jewish holidays are centuries deep and the Seder service carries a lot of emotional baggage. One need not be a true believer to be moved by the spirit of Passover.

Implicit in the story of the plagues which led to the Jews' exodus from Egypt is the portrait of an Old Testament God, as mercurial and passionate as any human. This is not the latter-day refined God of love, or the detached, indifferent *Deus absconditus* of contemporary thought. This vengeful God first sends a plague, terrifies the Egyptian ruler into submission, then "turn[s] aside and harden[s] Pharaoh's heart / ten times, Antagonist!..." He is a Pat Robertson sort of God, delivering divine retribution with a primitive relish.

But even as the children are told the old story, even as "[w]e pray tonight, dip herbs, and pour out wine, / forever what we are," I find myself linking what I call "our fetishes": the sacrament of the Eucharist, the symbology of matzoh, the unleavened bread, the worshipful care taken with the placenta among the Bakongans.

The stanzaic patterns in Part III rely heavily on rhyme and meter. Iambic pentameter prevails except in the indented lines, which are deliberately set apart; the rhymes are closely placed. The intent is to move the poem's expository passages forward without ever sacrificing the natural word order to achieve rhyme. Many of the lines are quite heavily end-stopped, which emphasize the rhyming pattern. I look at this and wonder how I did it.

Forty years removed from the composition of this poem, I have to say that I cringe at the first line of the concluding quatrain. Today, it seems facile, smart-alecky. But the motivation for all of these rites still rings true to me: We are all babes who suck at love together.

Recitations

In the spring of 1910, my mother, wearing her handmade best blue silk skirt, recited a poem called "The Curfew Bell" from the stage of the town hall in Radford, Virginia.

"England's sun was slowly setting o'er the hill-tops far away," she declaimed with appropriate gestures, "Filling all the land with beauty at the close of one sad day." On through all sixty lines of Rose Hartwick Thorpe's now-forgotten tale of a young heroine who saves her lover from execution by shinnying up the rope and stifling the clapper of the curfew bell that is to toll the hour of his death. "Not one moment paused the maiden, but, with cheek and brow aglow, / Staggered up the gloomy tower, where the bell swung to and fro.... / See! The ponderous tongue is swinging; 'tis the hour of curfew now, / And the sight has chilled her bosom, stopped her breath, and paled her brow."

Luckily, the old sexton who rings the bell each evening is too deaf to note the absence of its sound on this occasion. Cromwell rides into the story toward the end. Touched by Bessie's heroic deed, he pardons the young prisoner, whose name is Basil, and whose crime is never specified. Ah, Basil and Bessie! "In his brave, strong arms he clasped her, kissed the face upturned and white, / Whispered, 'Darling, you have saved me; curfew will not ring tonight.'"

My mother's skirt, which she had sewn herself, was made from material sent forty miles to Roanoke to be pleated. This detail was never left out of her retellings. Body English played a large part in the recitations of her day and the skirt, falling in knife pleats to the ankle, belled out satisfactorily around her as she writhed, imitating brave Bessie's climb up the belfry, up the slimy ladder. Then, as Bessie springs onto the rope itself and swaying through the air hangs onto the bell's great tongue, the skirt alternately flares and clings seductively to the prize-winning elocutionist who acts out the part.

This, at least, is how I recreate the scene. I can see my mother's demure onstage curtsy and hear the applause of her parents and eleven siblings, although, to my sorrow, I never found out what the prize was.

At the time that she confided these scraps of her personal history I was approximately the age she had been that day in the town hall. I listened grudgingly. What I wanted most in the world was to be totally unlike her. I had broken out in the itchy, surly eczema of adolescence. Immersed in Dostoyevsky and Saint Teresa of Ávila, I discounted my mother's verbal skills. Privately, I thought her a butterfly and a social climber, and perhaps she was. But she was adept at nonsense rhyming and could frequently coax me out of a dark mood with her impromptu couplets.

My mother lived into her eighty-fifth year, long enough for us to become friends, long enough for me to praise her ability to have poems by heart. I am grateful to her for the memory-genes she passed on to me. I'm grateful, too, for the adept and ridiculous rhymes, and for the nonsense language she often tickled me with, a gibberish that imitated the inflections of speech but conveyed nothing, except tonally; all useful idiosyncrasies for the poet.

I also was lucky in adolescence to have two pedagogues of the Old School as different from my stylish, modish mother as Rose Hartwick Thorpe's poems are from, say, Louise Bogan's. Juanita Mae Downes, my Latin teacher, battle-scarred by the Depression, alternating her wardrobe between the all-purpose black dress and a similar model in purple crepe, wore her hair in one of those visible-invisible hair nets originally designed for the kitchen staff. She was a large, square, ungainly woman in her thirtieth year of teaching *hic, haec, hoc* in the same public school system. She espoused not only the reasonable and orderly processes of conjugation and declension, but etymologized ardently and wittily along the way.

Tidal waves of this efficiently designed language and its root meanings washed into my life. Surely not the worst way to endure the seething introversions of adolescence, translating Ovid and Virgil, memorizing whole chunks of the *Aeneid,* the *Metamorphoses,* and *Tristia,* locating the caesura in each line and breaking the lines into their appropriate measures by scansion.

Arma vi/rumque ca/nō // Trō/iae qui / prīmus ab / ōrīs
Ītali/am fā/tō profu/gus // Lā/viniaque / vēnit
lītora, / multum il/le et ter/ris // iac / tātus et / altō
vi supe/rum // sae/vae / memo/rem Iū/nōnis ob / īram;

I muttered, marking the hexameter lines into their dactyls and double-lining caesuras. Long afternoons I stayed late to unravel the mysteries of the elegiac stanza with its alternating hexameters and pentameters, its diaereses followed by pauses:

cum subit / illi/us // tris/tissima / noctis i/mago
qua mihi / supre/mum – // tempus in / urbe fu/it...

It was better than crossword puzzles. Sometimes the subject matter grew racy: Dido and Aeneas in the cave, for instance. Miss Downes guided my endeavor, censoring nothing, for if it was written in Latin, how could it be unsuitable for a high school senior? Ovid – *Metamorphoses* in particular – got me through a terrible year in which cheerleaders and football players and planners of the senior prom (I didn't go) mocked me in my dreams.

In English class, Dorothy Lambert, as soft and powdery as Miss Downes was regal and rigorously corseted, shepherded me through parts of speech, the parsing of the sentence, and gloriously(!) the undiluted rules of prosody. Lambert's own Poetry Yardstick graced every student's copybook. Its measure was applied from metonymy to terza rima, from sonnet to synecdoche. Under her watchful eye I read Donne, Marvell, Shakespeare, Arnold, all with the same enthusiasm. Every week we wrote out another thirty lines we had committed to memory. A minimal amount of groaning accompanied this process; accreting poems was then considered a respectable pursuit and it began in grammar school. I remember in "Evangeline" my confusion over the "Druids of eld," which I took to be a distant place. And how these trees could stand "like harpers hoar" was an unsolved puzzle. For a long time I concluded that these were a species of animal, "with beards that rest on their bosoms," something like the walrus's mustache. In public assembly the sixth grade did the "Deacon's Wonderful One-Hoss Shay," or else Poe's "The Bells."

But in high school, pink, powdery, motherly Mrs. Lambert who was divorced and had secret sorrows, let loose on us masses of British poetry. She was mild and she was funny; even the restless, would-be dropouts at the back of the room sat still for her. "Would Sleepy Hollow please to come to order?" she'd say, and magically it came to pass. We wrote out sonnets by Shakespeare, Milton, Keats. Mrs. Lambert was much taken with the poets of World War I and put us onto Wilfred Owen and Siegfried Sassoon. In fever, I found Housman's *A Shropshire Lad* in my mother's bookcase and, without ever intending to, memorized most of it. After that, I fell upon Hopkins as upon a box of chocolates.

At Radcliffe, in Theodore Spencer's class, we again wrote out a poem a week from memory. On the side, I began to take in poems that especially pleased or deviled me – Yeats, Auden, Eliot, MacNeice – antidotes to the early large doses of Longfellow and Poe and James Whitcomb Riley. Sunny afternoons in the spring, on the roof of Cabot Hall, some of us combined sunbathing with reading poetry aloud, a dual sensuality I am no longer up to, wanting even the least sweaty poems in a cool, dry place.

My favorite professors were of course all male – there were no others, except for Maud Cam. The three I liked best were all foreign, either from birth or at one remove: shy Michael Karpovich, who had served in the short-lived Kerensky government; Elliot Perkins, who exactly satisfied my image of an Oxford don; and most wonderful of all, Albert Guerard. In my freshman year, Guerard, then a young instructor lecturing in the survey-of-

English-literature course, struck me as eloquent, witty, and urbane. He chain-smoked, which was then a delicious habit; he had read everything from *Piers Plowman* to T.S. Eliot, and he did not condescend to his students. Five years later, I was privileged to be a member of his graduate seminar in Conrad and Gide.

In the late fifties, when I began to publish poems in the littlest of the little magazines, then gradually in literary quarterlies of larger circulation, I met male editors who were taken aback by my poems, and the poems of some of my women contemporaries. As if we were some rare species of flightless bird to be sighted on special occasions. How dangerous we must have seemed, then! Undependable, hysterical; in short, female. And how tacky and sad this story feels to me now, looking back on it.

I remember my second daughter, age three, covering a picture of a merry-go-round horse lost from the carousel, saying, "Don't read that page. It's too poor." An emotion I share. In the early sixties, the published women poets could still be counted on the fingers of two hands.

Sometimes today on college campuses or at academic or arts symposia I meet poised, cheerful professional women who assure me that the women's movement is irrelevant now. They're terribly wrong, of course, but in a sneaky way I cherish the smug rectitude of the position. I admire their style, their briefcases, their credentials, the insouciance with which they cross a room, take up an embattled position in an argument, order wine in a restaurant, and make sure that the company's secretaries are not only referred to as staff people but are given equal opportunity to rise from the ranks along with the senior executive's nephew.

My daughters, both of whom attended Harvard during an era of coed dormitories, unisex bathrooms, absent parietals, and the bombing of Cambodia, have chosen more worldly careers than their mother. Perhaps growing up in a house full of intemperate poems and crumpled rejection slips, uncollated manuscripts and round-robin workshops had something to do with their choices.

But watching their yeasty comings of age, the long pull they endured to get their law and jurisprudence degrees, the noblesse oblige they exhibit in their public positions, I realize that they have, paradoxically, been models for me in my middle years. Who is mothering whom?

A jocular professor in an outstanding graduate program asked a woman Ph.D. candidate, "Are you ready for your oral exam? Good. First, take off all your clothes," only to be coolly advised: "Not only is that completely unfunny, Dr. X, but it's certifiable as moral turpitude."

Forty years ago, could I have said that?

And yet, I confess it, each of these daughters has taken me aside to say that the women's movement is too narrow, does not address the global issues. Hunger. Survival. The absence of hope in refugee camps everywhere.

Zero population!

Nuclear freeze!

Humane resettlement policies, immediate distribution of surplus foods; put that in your poetry, they are saying. Get with it, Ma. Write about the Love Canal, the challenge to safe abortion, food stamp cutbacks. Clitoridectomies. Poseidon submarines.

"'The great Overdog,'" says one, "'That heavenly beast / With a star in one eye, / Gives a leap in the east.' Remember that one, Ma? Remember when you used to write out poems on the breakfast-room wall for us to memorize? How we couldn't have dessert unless we knew the poem?"

Now *that* is a canard. The poems were chalked on the wall, all right, and changed fortnightly. They were to be absorbed osmotically, without any discussion. The Freudians have a term for this misremembered anecdote.

"'Loveliest of trees, the cherry now,'" says the other, dreamily, before I can defend myself, "'Is hung with bloom along the bough.' That was the one I liked best," then looks at her watch. She's late for a meeting, she's off in her running shoes, carrying her corporate high heels in a chic little box.

It's a comfort that they have poems in them, too. Poems, even imperfectly recalled, keep me company. My head is stuffed full of bits of poems from many periods and persuasions, and I am glad of it. In an age when creative nonviolence must stare down the nuclear first-strike fanatics, many of us may well go to jail for our convictions. Whatever the setting, poems are furniture in the mind. One I mean to take along with me is Marianne Moore's "In Distrust of Merits," for, as she put it:

> The world's an orphans' home. Shall
> we never have peace without sorrow?
> without pleas of the dying for
> help that won't come? O
> quiet form upon the dust, I cannot
> look and yet I must.

First Loves

In grammar school when I was in the fourth or fifth grade, Miss Blomberg exhorted us to memorize work by such sterling American poets as Longfellow, Whittier, and Lowell. Gold stars were given out to those who could rise, face the class, and recite flawlessly, or nearly so, parts of "Tell me not, in mournful numbers / Life is but an empty dream," or "Blessings on thee, little man, / Barefoot boy with cheek of tan!" or, in my case, a sizable chunk of James Russell Lowell's *The Vision of Sir Launfal.*

It is true that I had already learned by heart some of Robert Louis Stevenson's *A Child's Garden of Verse,* but these were accidental acquisitions from reading and rereading. While I enjoyed having them in my head they did not perplex and stir me as Sir Launfal did. The part I chose to declaim, at Miss Blomberg's bidding, begins: "And what is so rare as a day in June?" It is Wordsworthian in its romantic fervor, hypnotic in its exact tetrameter, and here and there, departs from its "June/tune" monosyllables to rhyme "glisten" with "listen," "chalice" with "palace." Of course I had no idea what a chalice was, but it sounded delicious. The "cowslips that fluttered in meadows green" were equally foreign to me; about thirty years later I discovered, picked, and cooked marsh marigolds, as they are known in New England.

But what gave me goose bumps was the description of the two birds, the male who "sits at his door in the sun" and the female who "feels the eggs beneath her wings / And the heart in her dumb breast flutters and sings." The concluding couplet tapped out its rhythm so satisfyingly that I felt an unreasonable exaltation: "He sings to the wide world, and she to her nest,-/ In the nice ear of Nature which song is the best?" "The nice ear of Nature"–how I reveled in the sound of it, and in the benevolence of this sunny, attentive mother. All was right with the world.

After my triumph with this twenty-four-line section, I went back and set about learning by rote the stanza that precedes it, the one where "The beggar is taxed for a corner to die in," and "At the devil's booth are all things sold." The cadences were the same but the magic was missing. "We bargain for the graves we lie in," terrified me and I quickly abandoned the project.

Miss Blomberg's gold stars were not the kind that are pasted in the middle of the forehead. Hers were solid cutouts, painted with a gritty gold paint. I treasured mine until the paint flecks began to fall off, revealing plain brown cardboard beneath. But nothing tarnished the sturdy four-beat lines so gratifyingly end-stopped that they thumped in my head. Nothing soothed me so well as "Then, if ever, come perfect days."

I think we internalize the poems we have by heart and they operate by osmosis to influence the writers we become. I favor the iambic tetrameter line, instilled in me by James Russell Lowell and sharpened by my later infatuation with Auden. Mostly, though, I am grateful for those old-fashioned teachers who revered the poems of a bygone era and by exacting from us our twenty-odd lines a week gave us an inner library to draw on for the rest of our lives.

PART THREE

An Appreciation of Marianne Moore's Selected Letters

Some time in the late fifties or early sixties, Anne Sexton and I traveled to Wellesley College to attend a reading by Marianne Moore. The audience was large and respectful; the acoustics were execrable. Moore spoke softly into a table microphone, which reproduced her sibilances but little else. Nor was the situation improved by the fact that she never raised her eyes from the page. With her head bent over the text, little was visible to the beholder but the famous tricorn hat.

Afterward, we stood on the edge of the crowd of admirers but decided not to linger, for we were merely beginner poets, students in a workshop, and had nothing to say in the presence of so lofty a personage.

I was sorry not to find mention of the Wellesley event in Moore's *Selected Letters;* details of her other public forays abound. The trips to Vassar and Bryn Mawr receive exquisite attention. The Harvard visits are thoroughly delineated. Did we invent the Wellesley evening? I think not; the memory is too vivid to be false. I was sorry, too, to find no mention of the visit Ted Hughes and Sylvia Plath paid her in Brooklyn. Its omission said clearly that Miss Moore was not taken with this young American's poems.

I paced myself reading *The Selected Letters of Marianne Moore;* fifty pages a day was as much as I could digest. More than this would have been like devouring an entire wheel of Brie at one sitting. I find myself considerably more sympathetic to Moore after this ten-day excursion which takes the reader from 1905 to 1969. While this is not a biography, the often lengthy and chatty epistles richly explicate details from Bryn Mawr schooldays to the glamour and fame of her later years, when she was lionized by the Academy and The Ford Motor Company alike. In the latter episode, Moore had been invited to name the latest model off the Ford line. She suggested every conceivable sleek and swift configuration; all, alas, were rejected in favor of the Edsel. Perhaps the Edsel met its appropriate fate; *The New Yorker* magazine published an exchange of memos between the commercial giant and the sprightly Brooklyn intellectual.

That she never met her father, that he is never once alluded to, either by her or her mother or by her beloved brother John Warner Moore, is scarifying. He seems to have been "disappeared" from the family constellation by common consent. Clearly Moore must have had some feelings on the matter, for toward the end of her life she managed to establish a relationship with some of her father's relatives – an aunt and a cousin.

It is the brother-sister relationship that posits a conundrum that will perhaps go unanswered forever. The affectionate intimacy between them as reflected in Marianne's letters to Weaz, Ouzel, Pussy Eyes, Biter, Toad, Badger, Pago-Pago (to cite only a few pet names) raises some eyebrows. John Warner Moore was one year older than Marianne. He had a degree from Yale, another from Princeton Theological Seminary, served as a Navy chaplain for more than thirty years and then took a post as chaplain at a boys' prep school in Connecticut.

Does his public stance seem somehow at odds with his private one? Without his side of the correspondence it is impossible to tell. But it is clearly significant that Marianne begged him to destroy her letters – invariably signed *dearest love* – or at least not to take them home, for fear of the jealousy they might arouse in his wife Constance, who is very scantily mentioned and then with great care. There must have been grounds for her angst; in the late summer of 1947 she and brother John are seen worrying over the division of their mother's estate. We are told in a terse footnote that the two siblings "felt Constance was concerned that they were arranging the settlement... in a manner that was unfair to the John Warner Moore estate."

—⁓—

Throughout the early letters to her mother and brother, Marianne refers to herself in the masculine voice, possibly not so curious as it sounds to our contemporary ears. Was it an equalizer to see herself this way? As in: "I play tennis every day now and am more the man, for doing it." She signs her letters Fangs, Rat, or Brother. Their mother is called Mouse, Mole, Bear, and Cub. From an early age it appears that the offspring are the parents of their parent.

While in college Moore boasted that she had had seven suitors but it was already apparent that she did not entertain sexual feelings for any of them – or for any subsequent men in her life. She was extremely comfortable with gay men like Auden and James Merrill, cozily at home with lesbian relationships, as Bishop's with Louise Crane first, then with Lota de Macedo Soares, and lastly perhaps, with the pseudonymous Roxanne.

The unaffected girlishness of Moore's response to college is charming. Cloistered though it was, Bryn Mawr represented worldliness as well as scholarship to her. The early letters display an athletic Marianne who plays hockey, tennis; goes canoeing, undertakes strenuous hikes. Incredibly, she chloroforms, then dissects a cat – this is reported with great aplomb. Her classmates go – horrors! – hatless and gloveless. She has an intense friendship with William James's daughter but it is not without ambivalence; an early example of Moore's feeding on celebrity.

Much is made of the crushes girls unabashedly had on one another. Moore is taken by a wealthy classmate to New York City, to Tiffany's, to theater, to hear Paderewski, of whom she writes: "He has that tiger-temperament, cold eyes and abandoned viciousness (in both senses perhaps), but I imagine as long as he lives he will not miss his kill." All sorts of new stimuli are provided by her wealthy friends. She is taken to art galleries, where she adores the Childe Hassams. She attends her first suffrage meeting; she announces that she is fiercely in favor of obtaining the vote for women, and of equal pay for equal work. Here is Moore in 1909, lecturing a well-to-do classmate: "Of course woman suffrage doesn't mean much to you, because you're petted and have money lavished on you and you wouldn't think of touching an infected horsehide or dangerous machinery for anything...."

As to matters of dress, Moore is meticulous, judgmental, and essentially vain. It is a matter of extreme seriousness that one obey, as John Cheever liked to put it, the sumptuary laws. The letters are peppered with descriptions: "Mrs. Lachaise in turquoise blue with turquoise blue fey and Miss Gregory in dark blue silk with blue hat trimmed with martin fur. I wore my black velvet suit, peacock petticoat, new turquoise crepe waist, silk hat, black satin and turquoise tie, and black calf oxfords." (I am unable to discover what Moore meant by "fey." Possibly it is a long-lost term for some item of apparel.)

Many years later, by train to give a talk at Vassar, she describes herself "in my azure dress seated on a new piece of cheese cloth I had taken along – with the left side of the blue hem folded over the right side, and my arms stiffly extended like a puppet's to prevent wrinkles in the sleeves...." And later in her life she receives innumerable gifts of clothing, dresses she could herself never afford, hats, handkerchiefs, scarves, even jewelry. From James Sibley Watson in 1959 a ring: "The emerald is of a color that disables comment.... It is like putting an imperial crown on a toad, for me to possess, let alone wear, such a thing – a dilemma – yet it might be safer for me to wear it than take care of it in the box...."

Nothing escapes her eagle eye. Gorham Munson "wears his mustache now with a small curve and tiny waxed points like a machine sharpened lead pencil." Isak Dinesen "has no manner, slightly smiles, but her earnestness and deep feeling shame effusiveness or even emphasis...." She wears "a tiny black hat with a pompom of black and white uncurled ostrich feather which threatened her left eye a little, like Skye terrier bangs." Elinor Wylie "is tall, spare, pale, with black shingled hair, rather wary and suspicious, with extreme intensity and energy of manner."

She skewers "Mrs. Gregory, a very troubled self-propelled poet & would be social leader – and Horace, thin, white, crippled with infant paralysis & a bona fide litterature." "Mrs. Warren... looked like these too beautiful to be true mannequin figures in Bonwit Teller's or Revillon Freres, dressed in powderblue velvet with gold slippers & gold & blue earrings, with blue eyes, and golden hair rolled and arranged as for a court painting." The envy and disdain, in equal measure, are palpable.

Eventually, however, her hyperbolic thank-yous for gifts of candy, objets d'art, tropical fruits, fichu bows, and so on wear down the reader. They are not only fulsome and cloying but the sycophancy becomes tiresome. Still, it could not have been easy to be on the receiving end of this constant parade of elegant gowns, capes, fur-trimmed collars, and so on, freely bestowed on her by her well-to-do friends. She had to perform an intricate gavotte of gratitude for their largess.

By contrast, Moore engages in tortuous convolutions, usually in the course of replying to gifts or proffering her own. One example will suffice: "When, as you will presently, receive a copy of my book, do not take the time that you are so much needing for other things, to send me word of receiving it."

Money issues could raise instances of wonderful testiness, as when she received the Monroe Award from *Poetry* magazine in 1944 and refused to go to Chicago for the awards ceremony. While the ostensible reason offered was that Miss Moore felt it unpatriotic to be undertaking unnecessary travel in a time of war, here's the rest of the story: "I SAY the check for the award should have CAME in the letter of announcement."

Possibly if it had, she would have made the trip, although she was quick to follow up this revelation in a self-justifying letter to her brother with: "Any symbolic or spiritual bequest *should* NOT be a big, external hullaballoo – and occasion for egotistical emphasis on clothes and personalities."

Nor is she above astute but scathing comments on her fellow writers. Archibald MacLeish's "very eyes are conditioned by the sense of promotion and benefice." Further, MacLeish treats her well "because he smells T.S. & Wallace Stevens on me." "Allen Tate has been a starved dog so long, all he can think of is breathing freely in a financial way & being among the elect." To Allen Ginsberg, she writes: "Your disgust worries me and I can't make clear what I mean without being objectionable... Soliloquize in this way over and over; people will not listen. What you can do about it, I don't know."

Sternly, to Ezra Pound: "I shudder at false witness against my neighbor and if I do not attack you, then I concur in it. Profanity and the Jews are other quaky quicksands against which may I warn you?"

From time to time throughout the *Letters,* Marianne Moore preaches from a platform of rectitude regarding individual behavior. "Duty and self-inflicted hardship as abstract virtues defeat themselves but when rightly applied, are the essence of perfection," she writes in 1921. "One is maddened sometimes into taking the wrong revenge." "Honesty – however dangerous – should be as valuable as radium...."

And her pronouncements on writing are just as meaty. "To put my remarks in verse form, is like trying to dance the minuet in a bathing-suit...." "I tend to think that every word of every poem should be as melodious as a Handel allegro...." "A poem is not a poem, surely, unless there is a margin of undidactic implication,– an area which the reader can make his own." "A sentence does not have to have a verb so far as I am concerned. Writing, to me, is entrapped conversation."

Her use of the comma is quirky but consistent; she seems to insert one before every verb, as in: "Your attitude to distance, stirs me." Or: "This perhaps exasperating volubility, is just to say..." By the tenth session of immersion in the *Letters,* her little stylistic tic had become endearing.

What ever happened to John Warner Moore's letters to "Brother?" Did he really destroy all of them? And when will we be privileged to see the other side of her correspondence with

Hilda Doolittle, Bryher, Perdita; with William Carlos Williams, Ezra Pound, Auden, and other notables? Eventually, I suspect, all will be made clear. In the meantime, this fat text is never boring and almost always rewarding.

This Curious Silent Unrepresented Life

INTRODUCTORY REMARKS TO VIRGINIA WOOLF SYMPOSIUM,
PLYMOUTH STATE COLLEGE, PLYMOUTH,
NEW HAMPSHIRE, 1997

Rereading *A Room of One's Own* has been a delightful excursion back in time for me. I wish I could be more exact about where and when I first came upon the essay that has meant so much to me. It would be interesting to research the exact year Woolf's works were cataloged in the august reaches of Widener Library at Harvard.

I think I first encountered Virginia Woolf's call to arms quite by chance in graduate school at Harvard in 1947 or '48, a scant four or five years after Radcliffe and Harvard had abandoned segregated classes and allowed us distracting females to mingle in classes with the men.

As late as 1946, however, the Widener Reading Room was barred to women; we were allotted a tiny, austere room with hard wooden chairs and a single table in which to pursue our labors. Books the boys could scout out on their own were delivered haughtily to us from the reference desk after a long wait. It would have seemed heavily ironic to be reading Woolf's essay in this atmosphere, but she was not in the canon then; indeed, it took another twenty years for her to arrive there.

A Room of One's Own stirred me and gave me courage, and I took it very seriously, but I did not laugh out loud at her wonderfully rich impertinences then. Now, fifty years later, in a room of my own, I chuckle, hoot, and roar my appreciation as I progress. Virginia strays off the path. A beadle comes toward her, raising his arms in horror at the trespass. She wanders to the doors of the library, only to be greeted by "a deprecating, silvery, kindly gentleman, who regretted in a low voice as he waved me

97

back that ladies are only admitted... if accompanied by a Fellow of the College...."

She comforts herself with thoughts of what once underlay this important quadrangle of greensward and massive stone buildings: "marsh... where the grasses waved and the swine rooted." Wonderful word, rooted. And then at dinner in one of the colleges "a plain gravy soup... One could have seen through the transparent liquid any pattern that there might have been on the plate itself..." followed by "beef with its attendant greens and potatoes – a homely trinity, suggesting the rumps of cattle in a muddy market, and sprouts curled and yellowed at the edge, and bargaining and cheapening"; to end the meal, "Prunes and custard followed. And if any one complains that prunes, even when mitigated by custard, are an uncharitable vegetable (fruit they are not), stringy as a miser's heart and exuding a fluid such as might run in misers' veins... he should reflect that there are people whose charity embraces even the prune." The dinner is totaled, put down, reduced to mere vittles. Prunes are demolished. She closes this passage with: "One cannot think well, love well, sleep well, if one has not dined well. The lamp in the spine does not light on beef and prunes."

But you know all this, all of you in this room, and you know this text far better than I. You know about Virginia Woolf's aunt who "died by a fall from her horse when she was riding out to take the air in Bombay," and that nothing further is said of this so suddenly dispatched lady who left Woolf a legacy of five hundred pounds a year forever. Well, more is said of the legacy, which came to her just as suffrage came to jolly old England and is, of the two, the more important to the recipient. But Virginia did not linger over this accident in sorrow, she did not eulogize this aunt, who might as well have been mythical for the rapidity with which she vanishes from the text.

I realize I haven't spoken to the topic that was assigned me, i.e., sense of place. Well, New Hampshire is not Bloomsbury, but our powers of observation are much the same. I would like to think that women writers in general are more alert to the nuances of relationships between people, but that is a sexist thought. It may explain Woolf's fascination with Jane Austen in particular, though, and with the Brontës and George Eliot. Inner landscape, that is. Surely the inner landscape is as important – I would hypothesize more important – than the external one.

For example, rereading *The Voyage Out,* I came upon some things that asked to be copied down and kept. Here is Mrs. Thornbury: "I spent six weeks on my honeymoon in having typhoid in Venice, but even so, I look back on them as some of the happiest weeks of my life." To be sick in bed with fever hardly constitutes the grand tour; Woolf's character strongly suggests her own profound pleasure in introspection.

"All around me," writes Virginia, "I see women, young women, women with household cares of every sort, going out and doing things that we should not have thought it possible to do." What would she have made of the ever changing and expanding roles of women at the close of the twentieth century? Yet for all her feminist stance, unremarkable to us today but courageous in her time, Virginia Woolf was averse to the wearing of trousers. She never went up in an airplane or traveled outside Europe. What a pity she didn't cross the ocean to see The Other Side, women in the United States. For all that she was reluctant to explore geographically, she harbored a vital curiosity about other lives.

Consider this, in the voice of a male character in *The Voyage Out:* "I've often walked along the streets where people live all in a row, and one house is exactly like another house, and wondered what on earth the women were doing inside... it's the beginning of the twentieth century, and until a few years ago no woman had ever come out by herself and said things at all. There it was going on in the background, for all those thousands of years, this curious silent unrepresented life."

You know the passage about Shakespeare's sister, "this poet who never wrote a word and was buried at the crossroads... She lives in you and in me, and in many other women who are not here tonight, for they are washing up the dishes and putting the children to bed." Happily, in the year 1997, a good number of men are doing the dishes, perhaps merely stacking them in the dishwasher, but tidying up nevertheless, and reading to the children and putting them to bed. Things are changing, slowly. I could go on and on about how things have changed for women poets in my lifetime. Our lives may still be curious but they are no longer silent or unrepresented. My hope is that I have offered my fealty to Virginia.

Josephine Jacobsen

Years ago, Stanley Kunitz said something I've always treasured (I am paraphrasing): "Youth is a biological condition, not a state of genius." Conversely, it seems to me, age too is biology; it does not automatically confer grace, virtue, or genius. And those of us who are old or older especially do not want to be reverenced just for lasting.

So the fact that we have sixty years of Josephine Jacobsen's poems contained now in her new-and-collected volume *In the Crevice of Time* is, simply, fact. And while she would not wish bells to be rung or whistles blown merely to recognize her eighty-nine years on earth, in truth her work merits the whistles and bells. I think we cannot sound them loudly enough in praise of this remarkable poet whose dedication to her craft has never wavered. I'd like to quote just a few of her bon mots about the state of being a poet from an interview given Evelyn Prettyman in 1984:

She said unflinchingly, "I have no interest in a poem which just makes a flat statement and has no countercurrent."

Her poems are rich in countercurrents.

She has said that writing poems is dangerous. "You're starting out on a journey in which you really don't know your destination. The chances are that it's not going to come off, that you're never going to get this nebulous, mysterious thing into language at all."

And yet, over and over, the "nebulous, mysterious thing" has taken shape and moves us.

When asked to compare writing poetry and fiction, she said, "In my heart, there is nothing that compares to poetry.... It's like a delicate operation. Under certain conditions you can't go that far in because you get to an organ that is a life source, and I feel that with poetry you get closer to that organ; I feel you're getting in as deep as possible."

Unlike many of us poets who share worksheets of a poem in progress with a trusted poet critic, Josephine Jacobsen eschews such exchanges. For her, the writing of a poem is, in her own words, "an immensely private occupation." And yet, once the poem is made and belongs to the ages, she turns Auden's statement on its head, for she believes that poetry can make things happen, though the change is painfully slow. So this very private poet continues to have faith in the public process and while she is not, as she puts it, "kindled by a poem with a purpose," she believes in the poem's ability to move us toward amelioration.

Josephine was born in Canada, spent her early years in North Carolina, and thereafter lived in Baltimore. Her father died when she was five years old and her memories of him are mythic and grand: she remembers scars on his face from fencing and heroic tales of his days as captain of a bobsled team. She was what we would call today "homeschooled." By the time she was sent to Roland Park Country Day School, she lamented that they were done with geography and it passed her by. To her sorrow she never went to college. Her Southern genteel mother felt that college was a refuge for girls who had problems or who didn't have, I am quoting, "a young man on the scene."

Josephine and Eric were married in 1932. I only recently learned that Eric came from a tea-importing family which went back to the days of clipper ships and was a highly regarded tea connoisseur. I was told that he could not only discriminate among the several tea plantations of Ceylon but could by taste discern on which side of the mountain the tea had grown.

The Jacobsens spent two months a year on the island of Grenada at the same resort, until it was "claimed" in the war.

That landscape figures heavily in Josephine's short stories and to a lesser extent in her poems. We meet mongooses and wild parrots, lizards; we attend a church healing ceremony.

Summers the Jacobsens moved up to the old frame house in Whitefield, New Hampshire, sometimes driving two cars north in tandem, Josephine valiantly leading, Eric gallantly bringing up the rear so that he could rescue her in the event of mishap. Although there are traces of the New England setting in some poems, Jacobsen was not a traditional poet of place. Her poems are portraits, cameos, ideas, most often lit from within.

Wherever they were, Josephine made time and space for her writing, but she did this so modestly that when you visited you came away with the impression that her sole mission in life was to provide a gracious setting in which to entertain friends. Sherry was provided at every lunch, and two mighty martinis with a twist preceded every dinner. When she was named Consultant in Poetry to the Library of Congress she said of the appointment, which provides an office and staff: "My ultimate place would be a closet. I work better the more I am confined and the less I am distracted."

Harriet Monroe, the founder of the magazine, first published Josephine Jacobsen in *Poetry* and every editor of the magazine from that time forward has used her poems. Her work has appeared in publications ranging from *The Atlantic* to *Yankee; The Nation* to *The New Republic* to *The New Yorker*. It seems to me the most distinguishing aspect of her poems is their clarity. From the very first group dated 1935 to 1950 to the most recent and perhaps most poignant ones there is a watchmaker's precision to her language, a surgical deftness that cuts to the specifics, and a passion that is controlled but ever pulsing.

I spent some happy hours this week rereading the poems in *In the Crevice of Time*. The leftover academic in me attempted to parse them, as it were, to place them in categories so that students might be told: here are the political poems from the McCarthy period, for example; here are the elegies, over there the love poems, next come the family poems, in this pile the colorful ones about the Caribbean, the ocean, and so on. Happily, this could not be done because of what I will rather crudely call overlap.

One grouping did announce itself, poems about what Lewis Carroll called wreathing and writhing. Josephine can be mordantly funny on the subject of the minor poet, at dinner. We see in perfect iambic tetrameter neatly rhymed how he "sits at meat / with danger smoldering in his eye," and how "By salad time, the very cheese / is paler, for his scorn and lore." This same poor dolt reappears in "Birdsong of the Lesser Poet": "Exuding someone's Scotch in a moving mist, / abstracted as he broods upon that grant, / he has an intimate word for those who might assist; / for a bad review, a memory to shame the elephant."

We all know him, do we not? As we know these figures "gathered in inter-admiration / in a small hotel room, to listen / to each other...," a poem titled "When the Five Prominent Poets."

When the Muse came,

> It was awful.
> The door in shivers and a path
> plowed like a twister through everything.
> Eyeballs and fingers littered that room.
> When the floor exploded the ceiling
> parted
> and the Muse went on and up; and not a sound
> came from the savage carpet.

Earned scorn is delicious in the hands of Josephine Jacobsen, but so is praise, as in this poem, "Gentle Reader":

> Late in the night when I should be asleep
> under the city stars in a small room
> I read a poet. A poet: not
> a versifier. Not a hot-shot

ethic-monger, laying about
him; not a diary of lying
about in cruel cruel beds, crying.
A poet, dangerous and steep.

O God, it peels me, juices me like a press;
this poetry drinks me, eats me, gut and marrow
until I exist in its jester's sorrow,
until my juices feed a savage sight
that runs along the lines, bright
as beasts' eyes. The rubble splays to dust:
city, book, bed, leaving my ear's lust
saying like Molly, yes, yes, yes O yes.

Last in this category, "Rainy Night at the Writers' Colony,"
this from her sheaf dated 1970 to '75, a small narrow poem
mostly in trimeter, the quatrains tightly rhymed, a rhythm that
always induces in me the delicious melancholy of an A.E.
Housman lyric – and I intend that as high praise. I'll read just the
first two stanzas:

Dead poets stalk the air,
stride through tall rain and peer
through wet panes where
we sleep, or do not, here.

I know the names of some
and can say what they said.
What do we say worth the while
of the ears of the dead?

This leaves me little time to talk about Josephine Jacobsen's
portraitures. She exhibits great sympathy for the old, the con-
fused, the unfortunates of every situation; the mad, the dying,
the deaf-mutes at a ball game, the Eskimo woman cooking with

heather, lying flat "to cook in a flat hut with a hole / in its roof. Blow! Blow! The ashes flew / into her mane, her red mongoose eyes." And then there are Mrs. Pondicherry and Mr. Mahoney, Mrs. Mobey, the Indestructible Girl of the carnival, the Night Watchman, the Limbo Dancer, the Blue-Eyed Exterminator, even the two men lost in the local woods. And a wonderful poem about the garbage collectors, from which I pluck these few lines:

> There are things here will go
> in the same slam and crash.
> Nor will she lie always
>
> on the pillow's fresh surface,
> hand curled at her cheek,
> and wait for the wondrous
>
> sluice of silence
> that carries the blundering
> laborious monster,
>
> its unseen men clinging,
> who erase time's disasters.
> Without moving she lies
>
> while the wings of great scavengers
> pass over the roof toward
> the hills of discard.

I feel I have not begun to say it, have not mentioned the poems in which death is subject and predicate, to be neither feared nor courted. Jacobsen is just as clear-eyed here as elsewhere. And she wants to be accessible, for as she says, "deliberate obscurity is infanticide for the developing poem." When she writes about the "first frost of sudden fall" she says that the dead come into her dreams as "freely as thirst to water" – an amazing image in this idiosyncratic sestina titled "The Gathering." And further, on the coming of winter, "The birds / take their lives in their wings / for the cruel trip.... summer / is what we had. / Say nothing yet. / Prepare."

No obfuscation here. And none in this review of "The Chinese Insomniacs," published in *The Washington Post* in 1982, with which I will close. The reviewer is Carolyn Kizer, who is possibly flamboyantly famous for her refusal to mince words:

> There is one further thing about Jacobsen I feel compelled to say, which will do neither her nor me any good with our formidable sisters: she is a lady. The dictionaries are not a lot of help here, because, male-written, they do not mean what I mean, obsessed as they are with rank and status. Piecing bits together from this source and that, I define it thus: she is gentle, tactful and incapable of cruelty, though she understands it well. She is the obverse of innocence, and more beautiful.

Back to the Fairground:
Mona Van Duyn

The other day I took Mona Van Duyn's *Near Changes* down from the shelf and gave myself over to the luxury of rereading these poems, underscored here and there in yellow marker from my first enthusiastic encounter with them in 1990. What I remarked then was her warm affection for the things of her world – an infant giraffe, neighborhood dogs, the spectacular sunsets that followed the conflagrations in Yellowstone, the light cast by a Coleman lantern in a log cabin, the homely dailiness of long marriage. All these acquire a special patina on reacquaintance, surprising me again and again with an outspoken quirkiness that deepens into exactitude as I reread and reabsorb.

Consider the flat declarative statement that opens "Falling in Love at Sixty-Five": "It is like the first and last time I tried a Coleman / for reading in bed in Maine." "It"? The act of falling in love posited in the title and never further elucidated? Instead, in loving detail, we are given a narrative of the lantern itself, which becomes a fearsome loved object, its "instant outcry" "roaring its threat to explode the walls." Further, "the lamp called out / the guilty years," it illuminates the book "in colors of lightning and thunder... in its artistry of rage." We are tricked into the plot of this poem, teased by the parallel episodes of blue butterflies and night-flying moths, and brought back at the end to "the speaking light" of the lantern. I chewed a long time on the title and its purported relationship to the text. Is falling in love late in life as tyrannous and brightly illuminating as the extended simile of the Coleman lamp suggests? As passionate and obsessive as the creatures drawn to the lamp, "the blind wanting that stuffed full each one's carapace / in a clicking crash at the lamp-glass"?

Perhaps there's a hint in the poem immediately following, "Late Loving," where we learn "'Love' is finding the familiar dear. / 'In love' is to be taken by surprise."

Reading Van Duyn is to be taken by surprise, line by line. She speaks of living "in double rooms whose temperature's controlled / by matrimony's turned-down thermostat." No sooner have I adjusted to that domestic metaphor than I am caught by an equally felicitous, outwardly prosy, wonderfully apt one: "Squabbling onward, we chafe from being so near. / But all night long we lie like crescents of Velcro, / turning together till we re-adhere."

The charm of these two poems resides in the imagery. Van Duyn is able to take the oldest and potentially most boring of virtues, monogamy, and freshen it with lively and compelling figures.

When she turns her attention to a mundane event in the outside world, she brings to it that same sense of wonder, this time coupled with terror and release. "First Trip through the Automatic Carwash" charmed me all over again as I reexperienced my own infrequent voyages through Van Duyn's. From the opening unexpected question, "Clamped to another will, the self in its glass / begins a slow, tugged slide, toward what clarifying?" I too am tugged in a childlike trance of terror and delight. I go from "Drenching and blindness" to "a fierce / forest whose long dark leaves wrap [me] in a wild / and waving threat."

The rhetorical question is a favorite device of this poet. Trapped, however voluntarily, inside the car as it is being cleaned, she asks, "What is whirling away? The long wedlock, / its bolt ground loose? Or the whole safe cage / of sane connections?" Indeed, these are questions the entire book raises as the poet struggles, like E.M. Forster, "to forget the India of the chaotic heart." And who else, reliving what I suspect was her one and only ride in a poem titled "The Ferris Wheel" could ask, "Does it remind you too / of the passionate climax, then the slow drift downward / into slums of sleep?"

Suspended in her chair in this same poem, Van Duyn sums up what has been her personal quest over a long and fully engaged life:

> Tell me how we can marry enthroned, imperious love
> to common human kindness, in order to live
> the only life worth living, the empathic life....
>
> ...
>
> (A last trip upward would be an anticlimax,
> the Wheel being too worldly to speak to everything.
> But if the stem should snap from a clumsy touch
> of Nature's overpowering tropes, let it be said
> that she counts on gravity to bring her back
> finally, and for good, to the fairground....)

A POSTCARD FROM THE VOLCANO

Children picking up our bones
Will never know that these were once
As quick as foxes on the hill;

And that in autumn, when the grapes
Made sharp air sharper by their smell
These had a being, breathing frost;

And least will guess that with our bones
We left much more, left what still is
The look of things, left what we felt

At what we saw. The spring clouds blow
Above the shuttered mansion-house,
Beyond our gate and the windy sky

Cries out a literate despair.
We knew for long the mansion's look
And what we said of it became

A part of what it is... Children,
Still weaving budded aureoles,
Will speak our speech and never know,

Will say of the mansion that it seems
As if he that lived there left behind
A spirit storming in blank walls,

A dirty house in a gutted world,
A tatter of shadows peaked to white,
Smeared with the gold of the opulent sun.

WALLACE STEVENS

A Postcard from the Volcano

"A Postcard from the Volcano," published in 1935, is not widely anthologized, although it reflects Wallace Stevens's ongoing preoccupation with weighing the ominous present against an ever more forbidding future. Here, he projects a modern Vesuvius or Mt. Pelée (or, heaven forfend, a second Hiroshima), a site of future devastation through which survivors and their descendants roam, sifting the rubble for remnants of our present culture. In this Pompeii brought up to date, children wander innocently over the hill, come upon the chips and shards of human bones and artifacts, and are unaware of their meaning.

Whatever the setting, the poignancy of stopped time conveyed by the poem is vivid and convincing. The two opening stanzas never fail to cause my neck hairs to stand up, however often I read them. I am in awe of the fast breakaway of the first line, an effect carried in part by the trochaic "children" and augmented by the short *i* sounds that echo, along with consonance, through "picking," "will," "quick," ("foxes,") and "hill." Transported by these initial sound effects, all my defenses fall away in the second stanza, where long and short *a* sounds are played off with the rolling consonantal *r* sounds. Moreover, the base line, iambic tetrameter, is just tight enough to control the diction without imposing stringencies on it.

Of course none of these devices – if we are to call largely unconsciously arrived-at juxtapositions of sounds and meter "devices" – would be enough to carry the poem without the hard sensibility of the poet informing it. How the newly dead whom Stevens has created regret all that is left behind them unfinished, treasured, yet stamped with their human imperfection! Looking backward from a destroyed future "Cries out a literate despair" indeed.

Even if I never know surely whether "budded aureoles" signify the halos of innocence or the early garlands of flowers, I will always see civilization's ruins haloed in this strongly rhetorical last stanza. The spirit of the creative artist is condemned to storm romantically through the ruins, railing against destruction, while, well outside human concern or influence, the sun paints the desolation a rich gold. How gracefully we go on bending the indifference of nature to human uses, and how insistently Stevens makes us aware of our self-deception.

Essay on Robert Frost

I suppose all of us who were born early enough to have one, cherish a personal recollection of Robert Frost. In mine he is quite an old man at the lectern – Sever Hall, I believe – reading his poems with the kind of authority and grace that goes with veneration. It is the era of crew cuts and Veronica Lake hairdos. The cast-iron statesman of poetry has already displayed his best-loved wares and turns now to a less familiar poem, delivering the lines with a hard edge. The last stanza is bitten off and spat out at this collegiate audience. Clearly, he is enjoying himself. Clearly there is lust in his voice as it quavers purposefully on *Provide, provide!*

Age has its own savage pleasures; perhaps chief among them is to admonish the young. There is a stone set in the gateway to an old graveyard that I visit. It avers, with a Frostian accent: "Stop, passengers, as you pass by. / As you are now, so once was I. / As I am now, so you will be. / Prepare for death, and follow me." So is the case made for our mortality and we are properly humbled. In much the same tone, Frost makes the case for expediency. As if to say, Since no one can be expedient to the point of choosing his own exit from this life, I advise you to get ready, prepare, provide for whatever dreary old age may await you.

I am generally uncomfortable in the presence of the didactic poem, scratching my itches, aware of a hot embarrassment beginning around the ears. The preachy poem is not unlike the pornographic story: however vigorously we deplore both social virtue and private vice, they can rise above their origins to delight us when they work. This poem most purely works. It manifests a Frost far from the Yankee farmer-poet role he has lucklessly been cast in, alternately praised and dismissed for his "easiness" – as easy, say, as Longfellow. "Provide, Provide" is neither optimistic nor orthodox. The lyrics illuminate unsparingly the terrible truth of man's nature. They express an attitude, as Jarrell has said, that "makes pessimism seem a hopeful evasion."

For everything will be taken from you in your fall from the fame that passes in our secular world as grace. What little comfort can be salvaged must be bought and paid for in full. But the poem transcends its bleak and stubborn honesty; it ends by delighting or at least gratifying us with its wisdom.

"Like a piece of ice on a hot stove," Frost wrote in a characteristic little dictum, "the poem must ride on its own melting." The poem must come into being, not without discipline and revision certainly, but arrive, a kind of hapless swimmer in the pool of its own sweat, unfolding by surprise, as it were. I would guess that the surprise in the writing of "Provide, Provide" was the way it fell for Frost into triplets. And once the stanza pattern was established, once, as he said, "his wordly commitments [were] now three or four deep," he simply got on with it, got on with the game of working through the meter and line to that brilliant, resonant conclusion.

Notice the word "simply." It cloaks the whole silent struggle of will that pounds feeling into form, elevates language to match the mood, and makes a straight way through the jungle to a strong closure. "Does anyone," Frost most ingenuously and rhetorically asks, "Does anyone believe I would have committed myself to the treason-reason-season rhyme-set in my 'Reluctance' if I had been blasé enough to know that these three words about exhausted the possibilities?"

It seems to me particularly fitting that "Provide, Provide" should have devolved into this hideously difficult-to-maintain rhyme scheme. To work in rhyming couplets in Anglo-Saxon English, even with recourse to approximate rhymes, taxes the poet and most often tarnishes his charm. To work in threes is to skate close to the open water of light verse. But courting this danger saves the poem from pulpit statement. The multiple rhyme does not banter, but it does swagger a little. The stylistic cut of it lightens the line and intensifies the irony. The felicities of the language prepare us for the consolation prize that is contained in a kind of Yankee glint. Stoicism, dignity, upcountry shrewdness...

And thus we are prepared for the regional alternate past-participle of "buy." "Boughten friendship" is salvation through necessity, a willed acceptance of the last chaos that life brings. It is not piety but a fact, a condition.

PART FOUR

XXVII

'Is my team ploughing,
   That I was used to drive
And hear the harness jingle
   When I was man alive?'

Ay, the horses trample,
   The harness jingles now;
No change though you lie under
   The land you used to plough.

'Is football playing
   Along the river shore,
With lads to chase the leather,
   Now I stand up no more?'

Ay, the ball is flying,
   The lads play heart and soul;
The goal stands up, the keeper
   Stands up to keep the goal.

'Is my girl happy,
   That I thought hard to leave,
And has she tired of weeping
   As she lies down at eve?'

Ay, she lies down lightly,
   She lies not down to weep:
Your girl is well contented.
   Be still, my lad, and sleep.

'Is my friend hearty,
   Now I am thin and pine,

And has he found to sleep in
    A better bed than mine?'

Yes, lad, I lie easy,
    I lie as lads would choose;
I cheer a dead man's sweetheart,
    Never ask me whose.

A.E. HOUSMAN

Trochee, Trimeter, and the MRI:
On A Shropshire Lad

About a year ago, while the medical profession rooted around looking for the source of lameness in my shoulders and back, I underwent an MRI. The initials stand for magnetic resonance imaging, a sophisticated method of viewing the human interior without X rays or surgery. An MRI requires the subject to lie absolutely still in a very narrow coffin for as much as an hour and a half at a time. Your head is held in a restraint that is quaintly dubbed a "birdcage." As they slide you into the dark tunnel on a slab, the roof of the coffin grazes your hairline, the sides embrace your sides. You are advised to keep your eyes closed in order to resist the claustrophobia that may otherwise overwhelm you. In some cases you are given a sort of rubber bulb to squeeze in case you panic. You are told it will convey a signal to the operators and supposedly an attendant will then extricate you (I never trusted this). All in all, an MRI is an aboveground trial burial.

Soon after you are entombed, the terrible knocking commences. A disembodied voice gives you fair warning: *"There will now be four and a half minutes of knocking," "There will now be eleven minutes of knocking,"* and so on, with pauses in between while they adjust the equipment and you lie enclosed, unable to move, anticipating. The sound is as percussive as a jackhammer and it is happening not down the block or across the street but exactly where you are pinioned. Like childbirth, or a turbulent flight through a thunderstorm in a two-seater plane, the only way out is to go through it, to endure.

What saved me during this ordeal was reciting lines of poetry. I have, in common with others of my generation, something of a memory bank acquired in an era when students were expected to commit poems to memory. Over the years, I have relied on this method with my own students, ranging from Princeton under-graduates who, initially, were superciliously disdainful of the assignment, to MIT engineers, who graciously gobbled up difficult poems by Yeats and Gerard Manley Hopkins and then disgorged twenty to forty lines on Monday mornings in front of the whole class. I tell the students who groan and the ones who do not that I am doing them a favor: I am providing them with an inner library to draw on when they are taken political prisoner.

My inner library is rather spotty and eclectic, ranging from selections from Robert Louis Stevenson's *A Child's Garden of Verse* and big patches of James Russell Lowell's *The Vision of Sir Launfal,* up through chunks of Gray's "Elegy Written in a Country Churchyard," passages of Arnold's "Dover Beach," a dozen sonnets from Shakespeare, Milton, Wordsworth, Donne, and Millay, several Emily Dickinsons and Robert Frosts, and best remembered and most useful during my MRI ordeal, A.E. Housman.

I came upon Housman's major collection, *A Shropshire Lad,* when I was perhaps fourteen or fifteen, and terribly susceptible to what Basil Davenport has called his "romantic revivalism." It is, actually, a synthesis of the severely classical – Housman was foremost a classics scholar who gave up the study of Greek, which he loved, to specialize in the later Latin poets, who were less well-known – and the melancholy romantic, an appealing combination when you are at the mercy of hormones and second- or third-year Latin yourself. His themes are somewhat limited: hangings, suicides, betrayed love, and early demise. Contemporary and universal as these themes may seem we would do well to remember that Housman's war, or antiwar, poems reflect British losses first in the Boer War of 1899–1902 and then, a scant generation later, in World War I. I think he could not have chronicled the even more searing events of World War II, for as destruction grows more impersonal, the poet's personal voice is commonly forced to go under.

At any rate, the first Housman poem I remember reading and adoring was an untitled little dialogue in eight quatrains, numbered xxvii, from *A Shropshire Lad.* The two voices are those of young men, presumably chums from boyhood, farm-raised and rather wholesome. The dead man addresses his living friend. Although war is not mentioned in the poem, we can perhaps assume that the dead lad – *lad* is a favorite Housman term – lost his life in battle, for many of the other poems in this collection are elegies for fallen soldiers. The plot of the poem is extremely simple: the living lad has inherited his fallen comrade's sweetheart. The fulcrum of the poem, the place where it turns and sweeps into its conclusion, comes late, with the final stanza, but there is a portentous foreshadowing from stanza to stanza in the question-and-answer format. Nothing surprises us in this poem. The drama is mild and full of pathos, riding on dramatic irony. As an adolescent female, I found it deeply gratifying.

Lying in my MRI tomb and doggedly reciting the poem against the terrible rapping, I realized what saved me was the regularity of successive stresses.

Before I define my stresses, let me say something about the traditional meters English prosody depends on. While early English poems were largely alliterative, as in *Gawain and the Green Knight,* stanzaic lyrics developed soon after, along with end rhymes. From the close of the medieval period, English poets began to take on French and Italian models, and with them the line of fixed syllables. But in English, unlike French, a word of two or more syllables almost always has one syllable more strongly accented than the other or others. To differentiate these, the convention of syllabic feet has arisen, the most common being the iamb, one unaccented syllable followed by an accented one. The poet and critic John Nims calls this "flub-dub," and claims it imitates the heartbeat's diastolic and systolic pulsings, which accounts for the iamb's popularity not only in poetry but in prose cadences as well. If you reverse the iamb you get the trochee: one accented syllable followed by an unaccented one. These two syllabic feet are called disyllabic because they consist of two syllables. Easy, right?

Then we have the convention of trisyllabic feet – three syllables – the more common of which is the anapest, da-da-*dum,* in which two unaccented syllables are followed by an accented one, as in "with the *wind* and the *rain* in her *hair*." The dactyl, its counterpart, is an accented syllable followed by two unaccented ones, as in "*this* is the *for*-est pri-*me*-val."

So much for our very quick trip through the principles of prosody, except to say a word about the terminology of end rhymes. When lines end on an accented rhyme as in "moon/ June," the result is called a masculine rhyme. When, as is frequent in Housman, the lines end with unaccented syllables as in "shatters" and "tatters," the rhyme is said to have a feminine ending. I hope that eventually we can find some genderless way of expressing this difference – Italianate rhyme is one such suggestion – but for the time being these are the conventional terms. Feminine endings lie a bit longer on the ear and help to carry the verse forward, masculine rhymes achieve a stronger end-stop. You will probably already have noticed that Housman alternates these to good effect.

What is striking about number XXVII, my chosen mantra against the MRI pounding, is not that it is structured in quatrains but that the poem proceeds with a series of unusual stresses hammering the first line of alternate stanzas. I scan these lines as containing four direct stresses and one unaccented syllable. You may call this whatever you wish: two spondees and a leftover syllable, perhaps? – a spondee being a two-syllable word with supposedly equal stresses, as in "moonlight" or "daybreak" – but I think the simplest characterization is just to say four strong stresses in a row. I cannot think of any other poem in the English language that does this, but maybe you can. I cannot find any other way to scan these lines, though doubters will try to force them into iambs and trochees. I cannot call up another poet who works so successfully in trimeter – three-beat lines – alternating feminine and masculine endings, or indeed another poem in which the voice from the grave enters into dialogue with the living. Since making this rash statement, however, a fellow poet has pointed out Thomas Hardy's "Channel Firing," in which the buried soldiers engage in conversation with God and with one another.

I think you can see Housman's artful shaping hand here, in the parallel constructions, "Is my team ploughing," "Is football playing," "Is my girl happy," "Is my friend hearty." But notice, too, the answering quatrains and how each one opens with an accented syllable, "Ay, the horses trample," "Ay, the ball is flying," and so on. I hurled these lines against the jackhammer over and over and prayed for deliverance.

As the MRI test continued, I found that truncated lines worked best to defend me. Arnold's "Ah, love, let us be true / To one another! for the world, which seems / To lie before us like a land of dreams, / So various, so beautiful, so new," simply did not cut the dinning. The exhortation is too lyrical, the plea too rhetorical, the language too rich with qualifications to hold up against such pounding. Frost's "There is a singer everyone has heard," also fell short, as did the Bard's "Let me not to the marriage of true minds / Admit impediments," although I lingered a little on how to scan "let me not," discovering once again that the best weapon I had in my head just then was the thwack of a trochee. I ran though my available Dickinsons on death, "I died for Beauty," and "I heard a Fly buzz – when I died."

These served me fairly well, both in terms of mood and brevity of line and even archaism of diction: "Themself are One," "We Brethren, are," "When the King / Be witnessed," and so on. Best of all, the lines alternate between tetrameter and trimeter and the music of four beats played against three not only makes the poem easier to memorize but reinforces the hymnal aspect, in the manner of Isaac Watts's "How doth the busy little bee / Inform each shining hour," which is probably where Dickinson acquired her sense of the quatrain.

Parenthetically, it is interesting that the poems I leaned on most heavily during my diagnostic ordeal were death-centered. In my temporary tomb I said aloud these incantations that purported to be about dying but wanted to defend against it. I concede that these poems are dated, both by the formal pattern of quatrains and by their rather lovely lugubrious insistence on our mortality. I confess that the tragic mood and underlying stoicism in Housman cause me to love his poems more, rather than less. The concluding quatrain of IV, titled "Reveille," neatly encapsulates his message:

> Clay lies still, but blood's a rover;
> Breath's a ware that will not keep.
> Up, lad: when the journey's over
> There'll be time enough to sleep.

Nobody knows where the notion of rhyming comes from, but anyone who has spent any time in the company of a curious child knows that the playful possibilities of the language emerge early on. Various abracadabras and fee-fie-fo-fums suggest that rhyming was an integral part of the casting of spells. It is a short step from incantatory magic to prayer and thence to paeans of praise and celebratory lyrics of, say, undying love. It is far easier to memorize a rhymed poem than, for instance, the free verse of Walt Whitman.

In the last hundred years, free verse has become far more widespread. While many poets have abandoned the rhyming convention, they still rely on other traditional devices such as simile, metaphor, and other figurative language, and most of the time they employ stanza breaks the way we employ the paragraph in prose. A free-verse poem may certainly be rhythmic; each free-verse poem sets up and reinterprets its own prosodic rules, as it were. None of this is exactly news. Milton eschewed rhyme in the writing of his solemn Paradise epic because he thought rhyming too trivial for the events described. Whitman substituted long, flowing cadences for rhymes, and did so to majestic effect. So did Wilfred Owen, one more flower of British manhood cut down in World War 1, who wrote: "My subject is War, and the pity of War. The Poetry is in the pity."

But for many of us contemporary poets, formalism is a way of life, a sustenance, a stout tree for the vine of our poems. We are, for better or for worse, committed to make rhymes, be they exact rhymes or slant. We are still writing sonnets, villanelles, sestinas, even pantoums and triolets, ballades and rondels, as well as inventing "nonce" forms to suit our uses. Practicing formal poetics does not in any way suggest that a poet is elitist or reactionary. Often a poet will choose to write in a historically powerful form in order to transform it.

Fifteen years ago, in an interview, I was quoted on the same subject. What I said feels no less true to me today:

I know that I write better poems in form–within the exigencies of a rhyme scheme and a metrical pattern–than I do in the looser line of free verse. Others can argue this point, claiming that free verse is a form and as such just as formal. But the harder–that is, the more psychically difficult–the poem is to write, the more likely I am to choose a difficult pattern to pound it into. This is true because, paradoxically, the difficulty frees me to be more honest and more direct. It is Yeats's "The fascination of what's difficult."

Death was much on my mind during the MRI—which, incidentally, turned up nothing. The correct diagnosis was made by a thoughtful general practitioner, and the right medication quickly did away with the worst symptoms. But death is much on the mind of the poet in general, which helps account for the profusion of elegies we write. We are all mortal, but it is the poet who shivers most articulately under the thin blanket of mortality.

ONE ART

The art of losing isn't hard to master;
so many things seem filled with the intent
to be lost that their loss is no disaster.

Lose something every day. Accept the fluster
of lost door keys, the hour badly spent.
The art of losing isn't hard to master.

Then practice losing farther, losing faster:
places, and names, and where it was you meant
to travel. None of these will bring disaster.

I lost my mother's watch. And look! my last, or
next-to-last, of three loved houses went.
The art of losing isn't hard to master.

I lost two cities, lovely ones. And, vaster,
some realms I owned, two rivers, a continent.
I miss them, but it wasn't a disaster.

– Even losing you (the joking voice, a gesture
I love) I shan't have lied. It's evident
the art of losing's not too hard to master
though it may look like (*Write* it!) like disaster.

ELIZABETH BISHOP

THE NUNS OF CHILDHOOD:
TWO VIEWS

I

O where are they now, your harridan nuns
who thumped on young heads with a metal thimble
and punished with rulers your upturned palms:

three smacks for failing in long division,
one more to instill the meaning of *humble*.
As the twig is bent, said your harridan nuns.

Once, a visiting bishop, serene
at the close of a Mass through which he had shambled,
smiled upon you with upturned palms.

"Because this is my feast day," he ended,
"you may all have a free afternoon." In the scramble
of whistles and cheers one harridan nun,

fiercest of all the parochial coven,
Sister Pascala, without preamble
raged, "I protest!" and rapping on palms

at random, had bodily to be restrained.
O God's perfect servant is kneeling on brambles
wherever they sent her, your harridan nun,
enthroned as a symbol with upturned palms.

2

O where are they now, my darling nuns
whose heads were shaved under snowy wimples,
who rustled dryly inside their gowns,

disciples of Oxydol, starch and bluing,
their backyard clothesline a pious example?
They have flapped out of sight, my darling nuns.

Seamless as fish, made all of one skin,
their language secret, these gentle vestals
were wedded to Christ inside their gowns.

O Mother Superior Rosarine
on whose lap the privileged visitor lolled
– I at age four with my darling nuns,

with Sister Elizabeth, Sister Ann,
am offered to Jesus, the Jewish child-
next-door, who worships your ample black gown,

your eyebrows, those thick mustachioed twins,
your rimless glasses, your ring of pale gold –
who can have stolen my darling nuns?
Who rustles dryly inside my gown?

Gymnastics: The Villanelle

Consisting of nineteen lines divided into six stanzas – five triplets and one concluding quatrain – the villanelle turns on two rhymes and builds on two refrains, which alternate. The first refrain recurs as the final line in triplets 2 and 4; the second refrain performs the same function in triplets 3 and 5. In the concluding quatrain, the penultimate line consists of the first refrain and the final line, the second refrain. Although some metric regularity is common, there is no set line length. The rhyme scheme runs A1bA2 abA1 abA2 abA1 abA2 abA1A2. A1 and A2 stand for the two refrain lines.

The villanelle came to us from the Renaissance, arising in Italy in the midsixteenth century, often as a pastoral tercet with musical accompaniment. By the close of the century the form had migrated to France and, in the hands of Jean Passerat, evolved into the model we know today. Largely ignored in the seventeenth and eighteenth centuries, it was revived by Edmund Gosse, who published his pioneering villanelle, "Wouldst Thou Not Be Content to Die" in 1874. Oscar Wilde also contributed to this form.

The villanelle soon crossed the ocean and was taken up by James Whitcomb Riley, whose "The Best Is Good Enough," published in 1883, was the first villanelle to appear in the New World. In 1897, Edwin Arlington Robinson's "The House on the Hill" further legitimized the villanelle in English.

In *A Portrait of the Artist as a Young Man*, first published in 1916, James Joyce has Stephen Dedalus compose a villanelle, "Are You Not Weary of Ardent Ways," for his old girlfriend. But it was not until 1952 that the best-known of all contemporary villanelles, Dylan Thomas's "Do Not Go Gentle into That Good Night," was published, just a year before the poet's death.

The fifties were a fine decade for the villanelle: Sylvia Plath, Theodore Roethke, W.H. Auden were all experimenting with the form. Contemporary villanelles by Elizabeth Bishop, Marilyn Hacker, Richard Hugo, Donald Justice, Carolyn Kizer, David Wagoner, and others continue to enliven this form.

Repeated lines in any poem have an incantatory quality. In the villanelle they become almost hypnotic, particularly in poems that are rigidly end-stopped and that employ monosyllabic masculine rhymes, as in Robinson's "The House on the Hill," and the rather wooden examples by Wilde and Riley. In Dylan Thomas's "Do Not Go Gentle into That Good Night" and Theodore Roethke's "The Waking," villanelles to be found in virtually any anthology, the end-stopped lines and monosyllabic rhymes, while still constraining, are employed to much greater emotional effect. Thomas's villanelle, hortatory and grieving, gathers power as it moves through one lyrical declamation after another. He calls up lightning and meteors, the expanse of ocean, the setting sun, all the while conceding that the close of day is at hand. To hear this poem recorded and archived in the poet's voice is to be made aware of the magical spell Thomas cast on his audiences.

Roethke's equally famous poem, "The Waking," teases us with its seemingly guileless simplicity – slow and go; there and stair – surely with rhymes as simple as these we can find our way easily from line to line. But what are these dichotomies, these contradictions, how does one "wake to sleep," "think by feeling," "learn by going"? Gradually we come to realize that the poet's subject is essentially the same as Thomas's: the ultimate journey toward death. Roethke capitalizes Ground, Tree and Nature. In a poem as brief and disciplined as a villanelle, we may read this as the poet's shorthand for deification.

Thomas's refrain, "Rage, rage against the dying of the light" may differ in tone from Roethke's "I wake to sleep, and take my waking slow" but the intent – the acknowledgment of our mortality – is the same.

Because English is a rhyme-poor language, many poets have resorted to the use of slant or approximate rhymes to extend their options. Some poets have taken liberties with the refrain lines, transmuting them subtly or ruthlessly, contributing a sometimes welcome elasticity to the form's challenging strictures. Hugo, in "The Freaks at Spurgin Road Field," has reversed the order of his concluding quatrain so that the first refrain line falls as line 2 of the stanza. Further, he has sidestepped the rhyme requirement of the triplets, contenting himself with some approximations – "night," "heat," "spastic," "quake," "worked," – and his line lengths vary between the iambic pentameter of his two refrain lines and looser lines that propel the narrative forward.

Elizabeth Bishop's justly famous "One Art" takes extensive liberties with the second refrain line. She is content to reuse the rhyme word "disaster" and to bend the remainder of the line to her needs, lending a refreshing colloquial speech pattern to the poem. Her first refrain line, "The art of losing isn't hard to master," holds fast until the penultimate line of the poem when it expands to "the art of losing's not too hard to master"; moreover, her selection of the bisyllabic "master" and "disaster" presses her into interesting, surprising, yet apt rhymes: "fluster," "faster," "last, or," "vaster," "gesture." These so-called feminine or Italianate endings entice the poet to reach farther afield for unexpected equivalents that will provide an emotional tension to balance the otherwise lighthearted chime of double rhymes. Also, the strong caesuras in the first lines of the second, fourth, and fifth stanzas, to cite the most obvious ones, and the deceptively casual enjambments in the second lines of the first, accord this difficult and demanding form a casual, conversational tone. It is a very different voice from the priestly incantation of Dylan Thomas or the mysterious hypnotism of Theodore Roethke.

In my own double villanelle, "The Nuns of Childhood: Two Views," I've given myself considerable leeway with the refrain lines, repeating just the tag ends of them where it suited my uses. I've bent the rhymes almost to the breaking point, too, always with the intent of achieving an accessible narrative flow while still playing the game by my own amended rules. The sheer sport of rhyming "thimble," "humble," "shambled," "scramble," "preamble," and "brambles" within the story made this poem a delightful challenge. In the second part, I went much farther with approximate rhymes, allowing myself to move from the feminine slant rhymes of "wimples" and "example" to "vestal" and then to monosyllables that carried only the *l* sound forward: "lolled," "child," "gold."

It's my thesis that we don't need to ossify these ancient French forms, that we can enliven and enhance them with the ingenuities of our own time and place. Perhaps in the twenty-first century others will remake the villanelle in ways as yet unthought of.

AT A PRIVATE SHOWING IN 1982

for Gillian Anderson

This loving attention to the details:
faces by Bosch and Brueghel,
the mélange of torture tools,
the carpentry of the stake,
the Catherine wheel,
the bars, spires, gibbets, pikes –
I confess my heart sank
when they brought out the second reel...

Anorectic Jeanne d'Arc,
how long it takes her
to burn to death in this picture!
When monks fast, it is called ascetic.
The film beamed on the dining-room wall
of an old brownstone
undergoing gentrification on Capitol Hill,
glass shards and daffodils
on alternate lawns,
harpsichord, bare board table,
cheese, nuts, jug wine,

and striding across the screen,
hauntingly young, unbowed,
not yet absurd, not yet insane,
Antonin Artaud in a bit part:
the "good" priest,
the one who declaims
"You are persecuting a saint!"

but does not offer
to die beside her.

And how is any of this
different today,
except now in color, and talky –
this prurient close
examination of pain,
fanaticism, terror?

Though the judges dress
like World War 1 British
soldiers in tin helmets
and Sam Browne belts,
though the music exactly
matches the mouthed words,
though Jeanne's
enormous wounded-doe's eyes
roll up or shut down
in hope, in anguish,
though Renée Falconetti,
who plays this part, was merely
a comic stage actress
and never shows up on celluloid again,

though Artaud
tonsured for the set
walks the streets of Paris
in costume in 1928
and is mocked by urchins
and is peppered with catcalls,
what does it profit us?

Artaud will die in the madhouse
in terror for his immortal soul,

Falconetti will drop out of sight,
an émigré in the Argentine,
we few will finish the wine
and skulk out on this spring night
together, unsafe on Capitol Hill.

A Way of Staying Sane

Most of my life-as-a-poet I have avoided writing poems about paintings, pieces of sculpture, sonatas, or other people's choreography out of a Calvinistic sort of purism, thinking always that to give in to the impulse to embellish another's art diminishes rather than enhances it. For how can the poet fail to encumber the object of the poem with adoration, or overlay it with private, not necessarily valid, responses? And then the poem runs the risk of growing claustral, precious, or turning into a mere intellectual exercise. Despite the exception that proves the rule – Auden's "Musée des Beaux Arts" – the temptation was one I sturdily resisted.

"At a Private Showing in 1982" breaks all my internal rules. It is based almost scene-by-scene on Carl Dreyer's early silent film *La Passion de Jeanne d'Arc*. The impulse to write the poem overtook me some days after I had the actual visual experience. I found I could not get the cinematography, the actors' intensity, and the brooding musical score out of my head. So I set about exorcising the entire event – not just the movie, but the setting, the social evening – by putting it on paper, a common enough practice. What I wanted to do initially at least was to come to terms with the movie's power over me, to go down into the maelstrom of my emotional responses to it – my physical repugnance to the fanaticism portrayed in it, and the sadism that fanaticism feeds – in order to discover what *else* the film was saying. Yet I had no sure notion I would find anything else. After all, I was entitled to my visceral response; wasn't it precisely what Dreyer had intended?

The poem began for me during a terribly barren time, which invested it with special authority. I was winding down from my year and a half as Consultant in Poetry to the Library of Congress, a somewhat embattled position in which I was sniped at several times by the right-wing princelings of darkness. I had spoken out against increased military spending, accused the Reagan administration of lack of compassion for the poor, attacked institutional censorship (the Renwick Gallery had closed down its poetry readings after some flap over a supposedly "political" poem), and cited discrimination in high places. This included the august library, where new appointments had brought the tally of men in the Council of Scholars to twenty-six, as against two women. For my offenses I had incurred the wrath of the Heritage Foundation, which cited me in their monthly newsletter as a pornographic poet. An essayist writing in *Harper's* magazine had mysteriously the same poem in mind. And, face-to-face, the librarian had accused me of abusing the hospitality of the library.

These digressive facts seem to me in retrospect to explain that my state of mind was rather more vulnerable than usual. I seized on the poem with a kind of fervor. It became something I "had" to write.

Something else was happening, too. More and more I was drawn to subjects that involve moral issues. I wanted to engage the necessary poems, not quite shunning the lyric form I love but bearing down harder now, in middle age, on the "eternal questions," as Dostoyevsky called them. I don't attribute this willingness to risk all to a surer sense of self but simply to the inroads of time. The lyrics will come of themselves, three or four a year. But the difficult poems, the demanding position-paper poems, are unpredictable. Thus the extra sense of urgency when this one walked on the set.

I dedicated the poem to Gillian Anderson, a member of the music department at the Library of Congress, whose search of previously uncataloged material had turned up the original music score for the film. A talented musician and conductor as well as archivist, Anderson devoted literally hundreds of hours to matching the music to the celluloid frames, rediscovering the synchrony that composer and director had intended fifty-some years ago. Because I had been unable to attend the public showing, Anderson and her husband invited me to the private showing that the poem describes, under circumstances that were surely more claustrophobic than the original screening would have been. For here there was no escape. A guest in their house, I felt I had to sit through my discomfort. We had broken bread together, drunk wine. I was enormously sympathetic to Anderson's labor. I couldn't leap up and flee. No, better to stay and faint from the pain if need be.

I am groping my way saying all this. I don't really believe that a poem deserves this lengthy foreground of explication. (And of course I didn't faint.) I would want my readers to be concerned with the words on the page, not with the poet's apologia, a kind of foreplay. And yet – and yet – is it ego that demurs and yields, all in the same breath? Now that the notion of audience has crept in, best to deal with it. Interviewers always ask: What audience do you write for? The poet replies with the solid arrogance of poets everywhere: First of all, I write for myself. I feel that I am sufficiently hard to please, that the first obligation of the poem must be to answer to its creator. Beyond this, virtually all poets will declare that they write for that "perfect audience of one" – the ideal Other Out There, who will be profoundly touched by the poem. I try not to think much about audiences. I worry that thinking about them is next door to writing directly *to* them, either down or up. Soon comes such a prickly awareness of the listener or reader that the poet begins to be swayed this way and that way, led into dancing the jig. From jigging to pimping for the poem is only a half-step, and fatal.

There is something else to be said about the poet's sense of audience.

Increasingly, the poems that we write are poems about the death of society, the collapse of the planet, the end of everything human we have been taught to believe in, to build from, to aspire toward. I use the plural pronoun because I think my moral dilemma as a poet is rapidly becoming every artist's dilemma. Thanks to modern technology, we can watch the world's local wars on television. We can see the torture and the killings in color, even as they happen. El Salvador is an example, but it is only one of many mind-numbing grisly situations around the world. What use do we make of this pounding on the doors of our perception, this battering of rationality? Why do we persist with our poems of anger and lament, even as we know that poetry "makes nothing happen"?

I write these poems because I have to. I wrestle with my own notions of human depravity in this poem, and in others, not because I think the poem can change our foreign policy, soften the heart of the military-industrial complex that feeds on first-strike-potential propaganda, or arouse the citizenry to acts of civil disobedience for peace, but because, for my own sanity (and yours, and yours), I must live the dream out to the end. It is important to act *as if* bearing witness matters. To write about the monstrous sense of alienation the poet feels in this culture of polarized hatreds is a way of staying sane. With the poem, I reach out to an audience equally at odds with official policy, and I celebrate our mutual humanness in an inhuman world.

In the poem under discussion, raw feeling was not enough. Had it not been for the presence of Artaud in the film, I wonder if I would have been able to complete the poem. He was the catalyst in an earlier poem of mine, called "In April, in Princeton," a very formal set piece written in matching six-line stanzas of three couplets apiece on which I had imposed the added constraint of finding a way to insert the words "in Princeton" in each stanza. It had begun as a kind of ornament, an act of fealty for the semester I had spent so happily in that luscious, wealthy community. But Artaud, whose work I had been reading in my big, bare office, invaded and saved the poem. To encounter him young, strong, and sane in the old film was a tender reexperience of the bond I had felt some years earlier when I read the sad drama of his death in the madhouse.

Gillian Anderson and I talked about the picture, too. She provided me with slightly erroneous information about Renée Falconetti. In the original draft of the poem I had the actress dropping out of sight in Brazil. *The New Yorker*'s eagle-eyed research staff saved me from this pratfall, however.

A word about process. At first I simply jabbed at the typewriter keys to put down everything I knew about the movie, the actors, my own despair, and so on. This is the way I usually work. Ordinarily, I don't feel safe about starting a poem until I have two or three single-spaced pages of lines, fragmented phrases, facts or imagined facts spread out on the desk. Then, I like to think, I can go inside and begin to find the poem. But this time the poem went through only four or five drafts before it congealed for me. The line length established itself early on, as did the loose "paragraphing" of the stanzas. On the whole, much less attention to form than to passion, except for my insistence on working in a short, even a staccato, line. I'm not sure why. Was I so involved in the film that I didn't want to impose any further patterns on it? Did the abrupt lines move for me somehow the way the film moved from frame to frame? Most of my struggle with revisions centered on how to deal with the chronology of the piece. Should the now-first stanza be the second stanza? (It was, through three versions.) Should I bring in Artaud later, much later in the poem? (Initially, he didn't arrive in the poem until after Renée Falconetti is named.) At what point should I confess I could hardly go on with the screening? I obsessed over this point, then blurted it out in the opening stanza. And the ending tumbled into place almost at once – a rare event, but one that almost always guarantees that the poem will be carried through.

The rhyming patterns in the poem are so haphazard as to appear unintentional. I'm not sure I approve of this new laxness, though I think it imparts an immediacy to narrative that helps propel the reader through the poem. I find I am doing this dangerously often now – "details," "Brueghel," "tools," "wheel," "reel," – and even "takes her," "picture," "offer," "beside her." This is breezy, freewheeling, associative slant rhyme. Part of me feels it should be legislated against, but the other, permissive part loves it for the easy flow. God knows where it will lead me, down what primrose path the old formalist inside me will now stumble.

I find myself hoping that this is the first of some poems that will take a new direction, engage in a dialogue with political situations, with moral concepts and contemporary dilemmas. There is no way to know that in advance. So I sit back like the old hunter, waiting for the bear to pass this way.

POEM FOR MY SON

Where water laps my hips
it licks your chin. You stand
on tiptoe looking up
and swivel on my hands.
We play at this and laugh,
but understand you weigh
now almost less than life
and little more than sea.
So fine a line exists
between buoyance and stone
that, catching at my wrists,
I feel love notch the bone
to think you might have gone.

To think they smacked and pumped
to squall you into being
when you swam down, lungs limp
as a new balloon, and dying.
Six years today they bent
a black tube through your chest
The tank hissed in the tent.
I leaned against the mast
outside that sterile nest.

And now inside the sea
you bump along my arm,
learning the narrow way
you've come from that red worm.
I tell you, save your air
and let the least swell ease you.
Put down, you flail for shore.

I cannot bribe nor teach you
to know the wet will keep you.

And cannot tell myself
unfasten from the boy.
On the Atlantic shelf
I see you wash away
to war or love or luck,
prodigious king, a stranger.
Times I stepped on a crack
my mother was in danger,
and time will find the chinks
to work the same in me.
You bobbled in my flanks.
They cut you from my sea.
Now you must mind your way.

Once, after a long swim
come overhand and wheezy
across the dappled seam
of lake, I foundered, dizzy,
uncertain which was better:
to fall there and unwind
in thirty feet of water
or fight back for the land.
Life would not let me lose it.
It yanked me by the nose.
Blackfaced and thick with vomit
it thrashed me to my knees.
We only think we choose.

But say we choose. Pretend it.
My pulse knit in your wrist
expands. Go now and spend it.
The sea will take our kiss.
Now, boy, swim off for this.

Word for Word: "Poem for My Son"

This summer, watching my six-year-old grandson conquer his instinctual fear of the water, I find myself remembering word for word a poem I wrote almost forty years ago, titled "Poem for My Son." The stanzas come back in my head intact, and the feelings that accompanied my writing it recur with the language of the poem.

Today I look at this child's father, a robust and hirsute forty-three year old who began life in an oxygen tent, and endured several childhood bouts of bronchial croup. Born into a family of swimmers, he struggled mightily to learn that although he was skinny and lacked the natural buoyancy of his sisters, he could indeed float facedown, add overhand strokes, and kick his way to shore.

The poem, in quite rigidly adhered-to trimeter, comprises nine- and thirteen-line stanzas; the final stanza, five lines. Throughout, the rhymes run along in a seemingly artless *abab, cdcd* scheme, with reliance on a fair amount of slant rhyme (hips/up, weigh/sea, and so on). The odd-numbered final line of each stanza rhymes with the penultimate line to form a sort of recurring coda.

I don't remember how much difficulty this invented form presented at the time. I do remember my determination to make the rhymes appear effortless, unavoidable, and perhaps not too obvious, for much as I love and lean on rhyme, I abhor the overt, in-your-face variety. And I certainly remember the relief I felt working within the constraints imposed by a three-beat line and a predetermined rhyme scheme. Once boxed in, I could say, it seemed, anything! Working in form has consistently been my salvation. I cling to it especially when confronting intimate subject matter – the death of a sibling, the love of a child, the loss of a close personal friend – for the demands of the schema drive me to a level of metaphor, an outreach of rhyme I would be hard-pressed to arrive at in free verse.

Recently, as my editor at W.W. Norton and I conferred on the contents of my *Selected Poems, 1960–1990* to be published in the spring of 1997, I argued for the inclusion of this poem. I feel it represents not only my early "tribal poems" of kinship but also the preoccupation with swimming that caused an early reviewer to tag me virtually amphibious. With considerable regret I finally withdrew it from the very small group of poems saved from my first collection, *Halfway;* there just wasn't room.

Now, looking back at "Poem for My Son," I reenter the struggle against the soft edge of sentimentality that I fear flaws many of my early poems. I have spent thirty-five years paring expressions of love and commitment down to the bone. Today, I would never permit myself the next-to-last line of the poem. I doubt I'd allow the easy vocative address of the final line. I recoil from what appears to be facile, even glib, in this ending.

While the first three stanzas still look clean and workable to me, when I come to the fourth with its presumptuous clairvoyance of "war or love or luck," I begin to lose my appetite for this poem. The statement that "time will find the chinks / to work the same in me," alas, feels not only obvious but self-indulgent.

The narrative content of the penultimate stanza, however, still seems acceptable, even interesting. Does one need to be a deeply fatigued long-distance swimmer or marathon runner to have experienced this ambivalence toward finishing the task? For the climber, even staying alive, say, at 22,000 feet requires prodigious effort. Still, giving up is not an option. What physical exhaustion teaches is, "We only think we choose."

One other small item of self-congratulation about his poem. I continue to admire a reprise from stanza to stanza, which I think was a gift from the Muse, for I was not conscious of its occurrence until well after the poem was written: in the last line of the first stanza, "to think you might have gone" is picked up in the first line of the second as "To think they smacked and pumped." The last line of the second stanza poses "outside that sterile nest" and answers it with its opposite, "inside the sea," in the first line of the next stanza. The penultimate line of that stanza, "I cannot bribe nor teach you," is answered in the opening line of the next: "And cannot tell myself." Finally, "We only think we choose" reprises in the first line of the last stanza as "But say we choose."

Perhaps without knowing it, these wraparounds were preparation for writing a crown of sonnets (see "Letters" in *Connecting the Dots*), where the last line of the first becomes the first line of the second, and so on. Reusing, rephrasing, regrouping a line makes for heady sport in a variety of forms from the villanelle to the pantoum, ghazal, and triolet.

And in a way, that supplies my credo when it comes to writing in form. I believe it is my option, even my duty, to rhyme without recourse to predictable love/doves or fire/desires; to remain metrically precise without lulling the reader to sleep with a singsong lullaby; to rephrase and reuse the line in surprising permutations; to play the intricate game of poetry by stretching language in all possible directions while at the same time compressing it into apt yet unsettling images.

Formal poetry exhibits freedom and elasticity within agreed-upon confines; as in swimming, you must let the water keep you and yet bend it to your uses. Thus, while "Poem for My Son" is not quite the poem I would write today, I continue to cherish it.

Scrubbed Up and Sent to School

"Subduing the Dream in Alaska," a poem I wrote some years ago, opens with a statement in which I have implicit faith:

> In the visiting poet's workshop
> the assignment is to write down a dream.
> The intent, before the week is out,
> is to show how much a poem is like
> a dream set straight, made rational.
> A dream scrubbed up and sent to school.

I've had good luck with this assignment in my own classes eliciting far-ranging and unexpected material. The results in the prison workshop in Fairbanks, Alaska, in the eighties led me to make a statement about our role in the Native American culture, a statement I had not foreseen as the subject of the poem. The wonderful thing about starting with dream content is the unpredictability of the outcome. While many of my dreams are too bizarre (sexual, scatological, or fragmentary) to serve as springboards, a goodly number have announced themselves as wanting further waking work, and several have risen up into completed poems.

—⁂—

Risen up, as mushrooms do, I have written, in "The Dreamer, the Dream," searching in my frustration to recapture an elusive dream's content:

> After the sleeper has burst his night pod
> climbed up out of its silky holdings
> the dream must stumble alone now
> ...

in search of some phantom outcome
while on both sides of the tissue
the dreamer walks into the weather

...

...and in fact he comes
upon great clusters of honey mushrooms

...

lumbering from their dark fissure
going up like a dream going on.

How often do we carry around with us the setting, the situation, the encounter – unable, it seems, to break free from it? This was precisely what happened to the dream encounter in "My Father's Neckties." In hopes of coming to terms with this ghostly reunion that nagged me through an entire day, I sat down to write it out:

Last night my color-blind chain-smoking father
who has been dead for fourteen years
stepped up out of a basement tie shop
downtown and did not recognize me.

Twenty-one lines later, the significance of our meeting "where we had loved each other, keeping it quiet" announced itself. The giant father of my childhood was indeed "a man who wore hard colors recklessly / and hid out in the foreign / bargain basements of his feelings." To this day I reexperience that sense of closure, even of liberation, upon seeing the metaphor that had driven both the dream and the poet.

—☰—

While my brother was dying of ALS – Lou Gehrig's disease – I had a succession of vivid premonitory dreams about him, the early ones rich with denial, the later, horrific in their acceptance. Just after his doctor had arrived at a definitive diagnosis (a death sentence), my unconscious had recreated my brother:

> Tonight he strides in rosy-cheeked
> and eighteen in the pectorals
> to announce he has six months to live and plans
> for every hour...
> ...
> ... Further, he means to kill
> time with a perpetual-motion cell.

That last detail is both tragic and funny. My brother, a skilled engineer, had from early childhood been a lively tinkerer, taking clocks and toasters, electric shavers and vacuum cleaners apart, sometimes reassembling them for their betterment. It was logical for the dreaming mind to envisage a way out, a perpetual-motion cell that would arrest time and with it the inexorable forward movement of the disease.

As his condition became more evident, my dream self began to come to terms with the inevitable. "Listen! I love you! / I've always loved you! / And so we totter and embrace / ... saying our good-byes..." in a downtown parking garage, this far a direct account of an evening all four of us, with our spouses, had spent together at dinner and theater. But I was in no way prepared for the content of the dream that followed what I intuited was to be our final outing as a family:

> At 3 AM I'm driven to such extremes
> that when the sorrowing hangman
> brings me your severed penis still
> tumescent from the scaffold
> yet dried and pressed as faithfully
> as a wildflower

I put it away on my closet shelf
and lie back down in my lucky shame.

My immediate association, odd though it seems, is to John Crowe Ransom's "Piazza Piece": "But what grey man among the vines is this / Whose words are dry and faint as in a dream? / Back from my trellis, Sir, before I scream!" In this perfect Petrarchan sonnet, youth and age, the life force and death are represented as the "lady young in beauty" and the "gentleman in a dustcoat." The latter emblem emerges in my dream as the actual killer, the hangman. I can't defend against the image of the tumescent penis, except to say that folklore holds that the hanged victim experiences an erection upon strangulation. (My brother was at that time having difficulty in speaking and swallowing. It was plain to see what was coming next.) In the dream I am awarded this token of the life force. I put it away as one would any other treasure "and lie back down in my lucky shame," ashamed to be still alive, lucky with the treasure of my own existence even as his is taken from him.

Reading through my early poems I am taken aback by the presence in them of so much dream material, so much detail "scrubbed up and sent to school" to make, for better or worse, the whole poem. My reverence for the unconscious is with me still, although I remember fewer dreams and am pricked less often by the re-collected fragments into working them into poems. Almost invariably, the dreams-into-poems have involved family members or very close friends.

"The Longing to Be Saved," a series of recurrent nightmares while I was housed in a motel in Fayetteville, Arkansas, one February, began: "When the barn catches fire / I am wearing the wrong negligee." The next segment dealt with rescuing my children, then my mother, and lastly my husband, who was home on the farm in New Hampshire during this wintry season when house fires are an ever-present threat ("I hold the rope as you slide from danger"). The poem ends with this curious reversal:

"Now the family's out, there's no holding back. / I go in to get my turn."

Although the resolution seems appropriate to the poem and solves the puzzle of the title, it baffles me as much now as it did during the composition. How could I dream myself running back (much as the horses do, in the opening stanza) into the flaming house? And are we allowed to astonish ourselves with a poem's closure? These questions must go unanswered.

But no dreams have been as vivid or lingered as long as the ones that haunted me after the suicide of my best friend and fellow poet, Anne Sexton. For seventeen years we communicated daily, if not face-to-face then by local or long-distance telephone. From "Splitting Wood at Six Above" – "I'm still / talking to you (last night's dream); / we'll split the phone bill. / It's expensive calling / from the other side" – through "Progress Report" – "Dear friend, last night I dreamed / you held a sensitive position, / you were Life's Counselor / coming to the phone in Vaud or Bern, / some terse one-syllable place, / to tell me how to carry on" – the loss is acute and the desire to reestablish contact (unsurprisingly, by phone) is urgent. These dreams, and others unrecorded, occurring in the first year or two following her death, find me not so much bereft as bewildered, not so angry as made desolate by the loss of our daily exchanges.

As time passed I was gradually able, I think, to express anger as well as sorrow. In "Itinerary of an Obsession," written perhaps a year, perhaps two years later than "Progress Report," Sexton turns up in a series of dream montages. In the first of these, "... here you come / leaping out of the coffin again, / flapping around the funeral home / crying Surprise! I was only fooling!" It's a bizarre scene that refers, I think, to the numerous half-hearted suicide attempts Sexton made before the actual event and seeks to reflect the mixture of relief and helpless fury that the rescuer feels in this situation.

In the next frame in Rome at St. Peter's Square "when the Pope comes to the window... / you turn up arranging to receive

/ extreme unction from an obliging priest / with a bad cold. You swivel your head / to keep from inhaling his germs."

The association to Catholicism is not accidental; Anne was drawn to the Church, strongly attracted to its ritual and longing for faith and absolution. She treasured her connections with local priests, one of whom aborted a suicide attempt when she called him (the phone again!) seeking forgiveness before taking her own life. This ongoing ambivalence – wanting to die, wanting to stay alive – surfaces in the dream of the priest with a bad cold. Even as she pleads for death, Sexton turns her head to avoid catching it, as it were. I am aware of my own ironic stance in this fragment, and inside the irony, my anger.

While I went on to write several other poems about our relationship, they are more direct, less revelatory, even, in one instance ("On Being Asked to Write a Poem in Memory of Anne Sexton"), written in the third person. The final stanza of "Itinerary" contains what I think is the final dream I built on:

> Years pass, as they say in storybooks.
> It is true that I dream of you less.
> Still, when the phone rings in my sleep
> and I answer, a dream-cigarette in my hand,
> it is always the same. We are back at our posts,
> hanging around like boxers in
> our old flannel bathrobes. You haven't changed.
> I, on the other hand, am forced to grow older.

The old relationship, grown bittersweet over the decades of her absence, recurs but now it contains a new element. Vivid, overt, and unmysterious, these fragments cohere to remind me of our separate mortalities. Sexton remains static, forever forty-five. I am assigned to go on with my life.

> Now I am almost your mother's age.
> Imagine it! Did you think you could escape?

Eventually I'll arrive in her
abhorrent marabou negligee
trailing her scarves like broken promises
crying yoo-hoo! Anybody home?

Virtually every dream example I call up out of my poems
teeters on the border between life and death. This seems quite
apt to me, for I feel that poetry is essentially elegiac in its nature.
We hold hard to those we love even as they die away from us
and we continue to pursue them, through dreams into poems.

PART FIVE

Keynote Address,
PEN-*New England, April 11, 1999*

On November 14, 1998, *The New York Times* carried, under the byline of Dinitia Smith, an article about two women resigning from The Academy of American Poets, an organization the article defined as "a venerable body at the symbolic center of the American poetry establishment."

Information about poets or poetry seldom merits mention in the *Times* – or *The Boston Globe* or *The Hartford Courant,* for that matter – other than on the obituary page, but in this instance the article ran to multiple columns and carried photographs of the two women in question, namely, Carolyn Kizer and me. A few weeks later, National Public Radio aired an account of the resignations, with excerpts from interviews with the defectors and with a current member of the Academy, as well as one emeritus member. Not long after that, the *Times* did a follow-up, as did NPR; then *U.S. News & World Report* called for further information.

We might anticipate the ongoing coverage in what I will call the poetry trade journals, *Poets & Writers* and *The Associated Writing Programs Chronicle,* which have been peppered with letters to the editor, all positive. Or, if they have received any negative responses, the editors have chosen not to print them. But what are we to make of the national attention? Was it a slow news day, or week, or month? Hardly. A president was being impeached, the UN inspectors were being ejected from Iraq, and the conflict between the Kosovo Albanians and the Serbian security forces threatened all-out civil war or even worse. Day to day, we are living through the prodromes of what may well be a Third World War. So what if two poets resigned from the boards of something-or-other? Wasn't it just some little poetic squabble?

Yes and no. Yes, because The Academy of American Poets is completely irrelevant to most Americans. No, because this tempest in a literary teapot is really emblematic of an ongoing debate in American society over how to achieve equitable representation for women, African Americans, Hispanic and Asian and Native Americans. Harshly put, it is not only poetry that has always been the domain of white males in this freedom-loving land of ours.

I have described elsewhere the restrictions governing my first part-time job in academia, teaching freshman English at Tufts University back in the late fifties. Liberal arts students in this required course were off-limits to me. The other woman hired at the same time and under the same tacit restrictive covenant – Alberta Bean Arthurs – went on to become Harvard's first woman dean, the president of a college in Pennsylvania, and director of a nationwide humanities program for the Rockefeller Foundation.

At the Library of Congress, when I was Consultant in Poetry for 1981–82, women heads of library departments were in scarce supply, other minorities even rarer. Between 1937 and 1981, there had been one African-American consultant, Robert Hayden. As of that date, I was the fifth woman named to the consultancy, a post which is now called Poet Laureate. "We don't count [heads]," the head librarian said to the press when this issue was raised at the luncheon announcing my appointment. "We do," I replied. Alas, we are still counting.

Two rather charming incidents from our poetic past – charming in retrospect, that is – come to mind. In 1937 when Edna St.Vincent Millay was notified that she was to be awarded an honorary doctorate from New York University she lodged a protest. "Not for myself personally," she said, "but for all women." It appeared that as the only woman on the roster for honorary docs she was invited to dine with a small group of ladies at the chancellor's house, while the male conferees-to-be were feted at a dinner at the Waldorf Astoria. And in 1953 when Robert Lowell puffed award-winning Marianne Moore as "the best woman poet in English," Langston Hughes rose to his feet and announced, "I consider her the most famous Negro woman poet in America."

Established in 1946 by Marie Bullock, the Board of Chancellors took shape as a self-perpetuating body with a rather vague mandate to act as literary advisers to the Academy and to administer the annual Fellowship. The chancellors constitute the jury that elects the winner of this $20,000 prize. In addition, the chair of the jury that selects the winner of the $100,000 Tanning Prize is a chancellor; the other judges are drawn from a list approved by the Chancellors. In 1994, the first year the Tanning was awarded, the winner was a chancellor. (The two other judges that year subsequently became chancellors.) In 1997, the award winner was a former chancellor, who had become emeritus a year before the prize was announced. It was informally agreed by the board that no chancellor would be eligible henceforth, but the bylaws themselves were not amended until 1999. (In March of that year, major changes were effected to create a more diverse and equitable board of chancellors. The term a chancellor was permitted to serve was reduced from twelve years, renewable once, to six years, so that what were once almost half-a-lifetime tenures are now merely senatorial in length. The three-person jury for the Tanning Prize has been enlarged to five, drawn from a list of fifteen poets and critics approved by the chair.)

Up until Kizer's and my resignation, there had been fifty-seven chancellors. Seventeen, or one-third of this number were women. None were African American. Of the sixty-four recipients of the Fellowships, fourteen of the prizewinners were women and fifty were men. Of the 121 total chancellors and Fellowship winners, four have been African American males. No other racial or ethnic minorities have been represented. (The composition of the board is now, happily, a mix of ethnic groups.)

None of this is exactly news. And actually, none of this is very important to the whole of the poetry community today, where poets of both genders and every conceivable stripe are enormously active. From my experience teaching seminars in colleges and universities as diverse as Princeton and Georgia Tech, Brandeis, and Florida International Universities, I sense that more women than ever are writing poetry today, both good poetry and bad, and the ratio probably corresponds to the ratio of good novels to bad, good memoirs to bad, and so on. The sheer quantity is very heartening.

It used to be extremely difficult for a woman poet to get published. Some women sought to clear this obstacle by submitting their work with nonrevealing first initials. If the playing field has not quite leveled out, it is at least far less lumpy than it was, say, twenty years ago. Certainly the situation in academia has changed dramatically. Now it is hard for even the most highly qualified white male to win a post at any university. To fulfill their mandate, schools paradoxically now seek all the minorities they once shunned.

Is this good or bad for poetry – and by extension, all the creative writing genres? Talent alone should be the sole criterion for publication in our ever more pluralistic society. But should we expect from our writers – poets and *other* writers, as poets are fond of saying – something more than encapsulating the lyric moment, some bearing witness to world events, to geopolitics, to global warming, rogue terrorism, and so forth?

Part of me wants to insist that the essence of poetry is contained in its lyric voice, that whatever takes place in the world as long as it lasts, there will always be a place for the personal cry from the heart. Take Sappho, or what fragments of her poems have come down to us – they are still compelling texts.

On the other hand, it is impossible to separate the life and the art as Victor Klemperer's *Diary* from Nazi Germany attests. Muriel Rukeyser, Carolyn Forché, Audre Lord, and Rita Dove have in common this poetry of witness, praised by some and detested by others.

I think it is precisely this difficulty of finding a methodology to encompass the new barbarism, this inability to locate a language that can express the new wave of elemental cruelty that has overtaken human behavior in our time, that stumps so many contemporary writers. Small wonder that the poets, especially, turn inward to look at the configuration of the dandelion or reflect on a grandparent's last hours in a hospice. As long as society appears as a given, and the poet's relationship to that stable, ongoing culture is a given, you can have Robert Frost proclaiming a bit showily that he had enjoyed "a lover's quarrel with the world." For the position of the romantic is invariably that of the lonely individual, intellectually, aesthetically, emotionally superior to the crowd, who elects as his mission to prophesy or to rail against his culture.

Writing in *The New York Times Book Review*, Adam Kirsch opens his appraisal of James Tate's latest book with this pronouncement:

> Strange though it may sound, American poetry today is more sentimental, more reassuring, easier on the reader, than at any time in the last 100 years. Not on the surface, of course: the techniques of modernism are by now deeply ingrained.... – free association, surrealism, complex allusion – [but] the modernist temper is gone, poetry has to a large degree resumed its 19th-century role as a comfort and consolation, a retreat from the rigors of the world.

I would defend to the death the poet's right to be inward, to explore his own sensibilities in whatever frame. But I find I agree with Hans Magnus Enzensberger, who says that the modern-day poet who shuns the real world, does so at great spiritual cost:

> Such obtuseness plays into the hands of the bourgeois esthetic which would like to deny poetry any social aspect.... [These advocates] advise poetry to stick to such models as they

have devised for it.... The promised reward for this continence is timeless validity. Behind these high-sounding proclamations lurks a contempt for poetry no less profound than that of vulgar Marxism. For a political quarantine placed on poetry in the name of eternal values itself serves political ends.

At the same time, I would add that we need to be careful of quarantines that restrict English departments from hiring otherwise meritorious candidates in their zeal to represent equitably gays, Hispanics, Native Americans, women, and so on. While there are bound to be excesses committed in the eager race for parity, it is my hope that sweet reason will eventually prevail.

I hope there is room today under the poetry umbrella for the polemicists, the romantics, the lyricists, the cynics, the ardently religious, the surrealists, the Language poets, the poets of the prose poem to take shelter together. Allow me to paraphrase from Anne Sexton a quotation I use, even overuse, with my grad students. "The writer," says Sexton, "is essentially a crook. Out of used furniture he makes a tree."

I don't expect our trees to form a fruitful orchard; on the contrary. Those who probe the innermost reaches of the ego will cast a cold eye on the political poetry of doves or hawks. Some will surely despise the poetry of feminist activists, others will defame the prose poem. The formalists and the proponents of free verse will have at each other. The dynamics of lesbian poets will undoubtedly be attacked somewhere by a straight critic, gay males will suffer the slings and arrows of homophobes. Atheists will be set upon by fundamentalists, light versifiers by metaphysicians, and so on. But we are all in it together, we who write poetry or fiction, critical essays or memoirs. Language is our tool and it is language that deserves our reverence.

Premonitory Shiver

It's traditional to open a keynote address with a few words of levity and this little joke seems particularly apt for a group of writers:

Mrs. Brown's husband, John Brown, died. The next morning Mrs. Brown went to the local newspaper with a five-page, single-spaced obituary. The editor read it carefully, then said, "This is fine, Mrs. Brown, but I have to tell you, there is a charge of five dollars per word for obituaries. You may want to shorten this a bit."

Mrs. Brown took the five pages back and returned in a little while with a one-liner: "John Brown is dead."

The editor read it and said, "Well, this is also fine, Mrs. Brown. But I neglected to tell you that we have a seven-word minimum for obituaries."

Mrs. Brown took the piece of paper back and amended it.

The editor then read: "John Brown dead. Red Ford for sale."

I am going to say a few things this morning about the public role of the private poet. By extension, I hope what I say will serve the prose writers among you as well, since poetry is often a springboard into those broader fictions of the short story, the novel, and the memoir.

It's now fifteen years since the late critic and essayist Terrence Des Pres published a provocative article in the *New England Review & Bread Loaf Quarterly,* which devoted the entire issue – over 200 pages – to the question of the role of the writer in the nuclear age. He examined in particular the response of the poets to the possibility of what he called nuclear wipeout. Perhaps we feel less threatened today by the menace of nuclear warfare, lulled into complacency by the breakup of the Soviet Union, but we are certainly at risk of global wipeout from chemical agents, bacterial infusions, and/or rogue terrorists who may have already created at least one nuclear bomb.

Here is Des Pres:

> We have fallen from the Garden, and the Garden itself – nature conceived as an inviolate wilderness – is pocked with nuclear waste and toxic dumps, at the mercy of industry and Watt [he is referring here to the late unlamented James Watt], all of it open to nuclear defilement. Generations come and go, but *the earth abideth forever* is something we need to feel, one of the foundations of poetry and humanness, and now we are not sure. That is the problem with nuclear threat, simply as threat; it undermines all certainty, and things once absolute are now contingent. To feel that one's private life was in the hands of God, or Fate, or even History, allowed the self a margin of transcendence, the dignity of personal life was part of a great if mysterious Order. But now our lives are in the hands of a few men in the Pentagon or the Kremlin [here in place of the Kremlin I will interpose Saddam Hussein, the Hezbollah, the Afghani fundamentalist madmen, and the no less malignant threats to the planet in general offered by global warming, acid rain, the vast burnings of forests and savannas across the southern zones, and so on]....We are, then, quite literally enslaved, and assuming that this bothers poets no less than the rest of us, why do they so seldom speak of it?

Is this a fair question? If so, is it answerable? Although I am one of the two poets singled out in this article as coming to grips in some way with the reality of possible extinction of the species, I am not sure I want to be so noted. Part of me wants to resist the raising of the question on grounds that the poet is no better equipped to wrestle the demon of ultimate destruction than, say, the dentist or lawyer, the flight attendant or psychiatrist. Part of me wants to insist that the essence of poetry is lyrical. And this of course is equally true for the storyteller, the memoirist.

At the same time, I am in a way begging the question. Given the social nature of language, which is to communicate, given the impulse to write the poem, which is, in Auden's words, "a passive awe provoked by sacred beings or events," the poet cannot escape his or her obligation to bear witness to the times. It is impossible to separate the life and the art. Nietzsche, in another context, once said that we have art in order not to die of the truth. Wherever there is language, there too stands the writer, the ultimate observer, a little to one side of things, but there. Whether the subject is a diving beetle or a firebombing, the poet's function is to speak of the encounter.

I will try to explain what I mean by the poet's function. Over my desk I have a line copied out from Rilke's Ninth Duino Elegy – in translation, I hasten to add – a line that so impressed me that I excerpted from it the title of a collection of poems. Speaking of the poet's role in society, Rilke muses: "For are we here perhaps merely to say: house, bridge, fountain, gate, jar, fruit tree, window – at most, pillar, tower? But to *say* them... to say them in such a way that even the things themselves never hoped to exist so intensely."

This exhortation to the poet to name things – to say out their particularities as clearly as possible – seems to me to go to the hearts of our "craft or sullen art," as Dylan Thomas labeled it. The poet's mission is to be authentic and specific; first of all, to evoke with an intensity that poetry, above all language by reason of its selection and compression, can evoke; the color, the clutch and hang, the shape of an event, an object, an emotion, a relationship. The poet trains for this evocation out in the world, conditioning, like an athlete, by steady exposure to the world around him or her. Everything falls within the poet's purview.

I have used the following anecdote any number of times when explicating a poem I wrote long years ago, a sonnet called "Purgatory," based on the unlikely hypothesis of Shakespeare's having conceived of his romantic tragedy *Romeo and Juliet* as a comedy – that is to say, a play with a happy ending.

We were then living in suburban Boston; our daughters were perhaps twelve and thirteen and I took them to a Saturday matinee performance of *Romeo and Juliet,* acted by the British Old Vic Repertory Company, then touring in the States. The audience consisted largely of students who had been bused in from high schools and prep schools around the area and there was a great deal of candy-wrapper static and popcorn munching; it seemed that no one was paying much attention to what was going on on-stage except for me. I sobbed audibly during the fifth act, which, you will remember, is very sad, involving the deaths of the lovers. When the curtain fell and the houselights came up, my two daughters went out on either side of me to the aisle and pretended they had no connection to this demented woman. On the way home, the kinder one said, "It was only a play, Mother," and the less kind one said, "I have never been so humiliated in my life."

Here is the poem, a Shakespearean sonnet:

> And suppose the darlings get to Mantua,
> suppose they cheat the crypt, what next? Begin
> with him, unshaven. Though not, I grant you, a
> displeasing cockerel, there's egg yolk on his chin.
> His seedy robe's aflap, he's got the rheum.
> Poor dear, the cooking lard has smoked her eye.
> Another Montague is in the womb
> although the first babe's bottom's not yet dry.
> She scrolls a weekly letter to her Nurse

who dares to send a smock through Balthasar,
and once a month, his father posts a purse.
News from Verona? Always news of war.
    Such sour years it takes to right this wrong:
    The fifth act runs unconscionably long.

Granted, the poem is bearing witness to another time, a time of civil war and familial rivalry between the Montagues and the Capulets. But the emotion Shakespeare evoked is certainly universal and ubiquitous. And in spite of the humor implicit in my rewrite of the tale, the message, in any age or setting, remains: News from Verona? Always news of war.

Everything I have said applies here also to the prose writer. I've recently been reading excerpts from *I Will Bear Witness,* excerpted in *The New Yorker* magazine. Victor Klemperer was a German Jew, a decorated veteran of the First World War, who converted to Protestantism, married a Protestant, and was a distinguished professor of French literature at the time that Hitler came to power. Klemperer and his wife delayed leaving Nazi Germany until it was no longer possible to emigrate, and Klemperer began to record faithfully, in longhand, not, as he says, a "history, but simply to bear witness to the everyday life of tyranny." That, he said, was his heroism. Remarkably, the diaries survived, as did Victor Klemperer; survived the Dresden bombing, vividly described, survived arrest and imprisonment, survived the extermination of everyone around him. So that we have an unsentimental unself-pitying account of the dailiness of life in the Third Reich, something we can see as a coda to Anne Frank's diary, which breaks off when the Franks are seized and deported to the concentration camp. Klemperer's entries take us through and beyond.

Well, one doesn't have to endure life in a dictatorship to become a writer – Klemperer, in fact, never saw himself as a writer, merely a secretary of the terrible events unfolding as the years passed – but to have moved beyond the academic cloister into a workaday world will inevitably prove useful to the beginner. For this reason, I always encourage talented college seniors to take time away from the groves of academe before sliding into an MFA program at Iowa or Arkansas or Columbia. I urge them to find work in a hospital, drive a taxi, sell brushes and brooms, clean motel rooms, but pursue the holy arts of seeing, feeling, and naming out in the real world.

I once spent a very pleasant half-hour backstage talking about wild mushrooms with Czeslaw Milosz, whom I was to introduce to an audience at the Library of Congress. I had never met him before that somewhat awkward bringing together in an airless little room to one side of the apron. What might have been a painfully stiff period of waiting for the rustling assemblage to find its seats out front in the auditorium was made delightful by the fact that we had something very specific in common beyond our commitment to poetry. Although we came from two different cultures, two separate geographies, we both had walked the forest floor with our baskets. An ocean had flowed between our foragings, but we shared the same Latin nomenclature and recognition system. This despite the fact that classification systems for the thousands of fungi are constantly changing. House, bridge, fountain, gate – *armillaria (now armillariella) mellea, russula, lepiota procera, agaricus campestris*. The joy of naming! In the process of naming, the poet can impose a degree of order on the chaos of events and of feelings that surface and demand his or her attention. And this brings us back to my ambivalence about Des Pres's question.

It is not so simple a matter as asking the poem to preach, take a stand, rise up on a soapbox in Hyde Park or Postoffice Square. That would be a dreadful reductivism, requiring the poet to suppress the private, the personal, indeed the most critical aspect of his/her being. Of course the contemporary poem is informed by a consciousness of the milieu that shapes it. It cannot be otherwise in this complicated age where we must confront the urgent possibility of holocaust by bomb, nerve gas, anthrax or other agent, the collapse of the planet, the death of society, the end of everything human we have grown up believing in. But the driving force of the poem, the direction the poet takes is an internal matter. If our detachment, our cynicism or political naïveté, is undergoing a change, it is because our identities and the relationship of our identities to the culture are changing as well.

When Robert Frost spoke of having picked "a lover's quarrel with the world," it was a stable and secure world he remonstrated with. It was at least a world with the certainty of ongoingness still accepted as commonplace.

> And were an epitaph to be my story
> I'd have a short one ready for my own.
> I would have written of me on my stone:
> I had a lover's quarrel with the world.

For an epitaph presumes a new generation to visit the cemetery. There is perpetual care behind this little quatrain of his.

That order no longer obtains. Prophetically, some thirty years earlier, Yeats could write:

> Turning and turning in the widening gyre
> The falcon cannot hear the falconer;
> Things fall apart; the center cannot hold...

These are the opening lines from Yeats's famous poem "The Second Coming," the poem that ends with the image that still raises gooseflesh for a generation of new readers:

> And what rough beast, its hour come round at last,
> Slouches towards Bethlehem to be born?

The fact that Joan Didion titled a collection of essays on contemporary life and letters *Slouching Towards Bethlehem* says something about the power of Yeats's vision. He wrote that poem in the dark despairing year of 1919, an era at the close of the First World War that looks to us now like a bright beacon shining in a world still ruled by a humane cultural tradition, a world that still gave lip service at least to the Judeo-Christian ethic.

Exactly twenty years later, sitting, "in one of the dives / On Fifty-second Street" as he put it, an English expatriate named Wystan Auden wrote another cry from the heart predicated on that ethic. The poem, titled "September 1, 1939," was initiated by the Nazi invasion of Poland, which signaled the beginning of World War II. Perhaps because in his rising pessimism he felt that the poem's most direct dogmatic statement was not possible, or because he shunned the didacticism inherent in it, Auden omitted the penultimate stanza from the poem in its later reprintings. In particular, the line he wanted excised reads "We must love one another or die." Many anthologies subsequently acceded to his demand and chopped out the offending stanza, which I should now like to quote in full:

> All I have is a voice
> To undo the folded lie,
> The romantic lie in the brain
> Of the sensual man-in-the-street
> And the lie of Authority
> Whose buildings grope the sky:
> There is no such thing as the State
> And no one exists alone;
> Hunger allows no Choice
> To the citizen or the police;
> We must love one another or die.

Auden closes this poem on a note of humility and prayer. I think of it as a self-prayer, the "May I" addressed to his own soul.

> May I, composed like them
> Of Eros and of dust,

Beleaguered by the same
Negation and despair,
Show an affirming flame.

The "affirming flame" has continued to shine out of much of
the poetry of our century, or did so at least until the onset of the
nuclear age. This poem of Auden's and subsequent poems – in
particular the long sequence from Auden's *The Double Man* titled
"New Year's Letter" – the poems of MacNeice and Spender,
Marianne Moore's "In Distrust of Merits," the poems of the re-
markable British poet-historians of World War I, Owen, Sassoon,
and Brooke; indeed the American poet-historians of World War
II, Shapiro and Jarrell, Dickey and Eberhart, all presume that the
cataclysm of global war is an aberration, a mistake.

Cyril Connolly, writing in the English magazine *Horizon*
early in World War II, went much further. He said – and how
ridiculous this sounds to our ears today – "War is the enemy of
creative activity and writers are wise to ignore it and concentrate
on other subjects." A soldier-poet (how well this exchange illus-
trates that there will always be an England) writing back, dis-
agreed strongly, saying of the poet that:

> It is his duty to show that even in war humanity
> may be crucified, but does not die. I do not know
> if there are artists alive today who can achieve
> this triumph, but if there are, I am certain they
> will see in the war, as artists once saw in the cru-
> cifixion of Christ, not only one more squalid in-
> cident in the interminable suicide of humanity,
> but tragic and terrible birth.

"You would think the fury of aerial bombardment / Would
rouse God to relent," Richard Eberhart could write in the
1940s. Randall Jarrell put it this way: "In bombers named for
girls, we burned / The cities we had learned about in school...."

In "Elegy for a Dead Soldier," Karl Shapiro wrote:

> His children would have known a heritage,
> Just or unjust, the richest in the world,
> The quantum of all art and science curled
> In the horn of plenty, bursting from the horn,
> A people bathed in honey...

It seems to me that there is a kind of optimism implicit in the informing innocence of these lines. Underlying them are presumptions about goodness and progress, about freedom from fear and want and the rest, none of which can be called on today.

Perhaps first in Jarrell's "Death of the Ball Turret Gunner" does a chilling prescience occur. The gunner, a hapless contemporary victim who goes from one fetal position to another, speaks:

> From my mother's sleep I fell into the State,
> And I hunched in its belly till my wet fur froze.
> Six miles from earth, loosed from its dream of life,
> I woke to black flak and the nightmare fighters.
> When I died they washed me out of the turret with
>   a hose.

Faced with that fall "into the State," faced with a splintering world, perhaps it is true that American poetry, post–World War II, has grown increasingly small-themed and introspective. Des Pres in his article says he is struck by contemporary poetry's sameness, huddled stance, meagerness. What shocks him is "the completeness, the sealed-up way these poems deny the knowledge or the nearness of nuclear threat."

Part of this tacit decision not to come to grips with the overwhelming issue of the era arises, ironically enough, out of an instinct for self-preservation. The subject, it is argued, is too big, too important to be tackled in a poem or short story. It is unwieldy, defeating, futile for the writer to attempt to deal with the final big bang and its implications. It is futile to stand in protest against it, for of what use are protest poems? They are read only by the already converted.

What use was the read-in, for instance, when on November 11, Armistice Day, 1984, a hundred or so New England poets staged a poetry-thon around the clock in a Cambridge, Massachusetts, church to express their solidarity for a nuclear freeze? Why not content ourselves, going down the long slide together, with landscape poems, love poems, poems that say aloud I Who Me, I Who Me! into the final blast?

Donald Hall, looking at the plateau-like sameness of many contemporary poems, dubbed them McPoems, cloned out of MFA programs where line breaks, amount of white spaces around the lines, and narrow connotative shifts of meanings can usurp hours of a group's attention.

And, while I am playing devil's advocate, what possible difference can any of this make in the grand scheme of things? Nobody listens to poets anymore in this country, except marginally during Poetry Month when C-Span covers the gala at the White House. Television is king, fast foods are our sustenance, and you can even get your hour of God per week at the drive-in church. In truth, nobody reads poetry except other poets and a few students and a sprinkling of academics and eccentrics. People claim they don't read poetry because it is too difficult or obscure – a favorite condemnation.

Jarrell has a lively essay on this matter, an essay which is more than thirty years old but sounds as contemporary as Windows 98.

> People who have inherited the custom of not reading poets justify it by referring to the obscurity of the poems they have never read – since most people decide that poets are obscure very much as legislators decide that books are pornographic – by glancing at a few fragments someone

has strung together to disgust them.... The man who monthly reads, with vacant relish, the carefully predigested sentences which the *Reader's Digest* feeds to him as a mother pigeon feeds her squabs – this man *cannot* read *The Divine Comedy*, even if it should occur to him to try; it is too obscure. Yet one sort of clearness shows a complete contempt for the reader, just as one sort of obscurity shows a complete respect. Which patronizes and degrades the reader, *The Divine Comedy* with its four levels of meaning, or the *Reader's Digest* with its one level sunk so low that it seems not a level but an abyss into which the reader consents to sink? The writer's real dishonesty is to give an easy paraphrase of the hard truth.

So, on the one hand, we have the unread because of the unreadable contemporary poet, who is angry and unwilling to submit to his obscurity. On the other, we have a tacit acknowledgment among poets that we cannot bring back, in Jarrell's words, "that Yesterday in which people stood on chairs to look at Lord Tennyson." We have a society in which the poet is perceived, at least by the midculture, our *Reader's Digest* consumer, as a fop, a weakling, an innocent dweller in ivory towers, a possibly lovable but fuzzy, absentminded philosopher, a unicycle rider sharing the tightrope with a trained bear.

Of course the poet is not alone in his obscurity. At a conference held at UCLA to bring American and Chinese writers together in dialogue for the first time, Kurt Vonnegut insisted that writers in America have about as much social impact as a pancake falling from a height of four feet. Later he did admit that if he didn't believe writers had some impact on their times he would have become an optometrist instead. "Here in America," Vonnegut said, "for 200 years we have been allowed to say whatever we want to, as loud as we want – and politicians are wholly unafraid of us."

Arthur Miller, speaking to this point, said he didn't think any writer wrote because he considered writing a social function. This disclaimer from a playwright who has consistently grappled with large social issues seems rather modest as well as contradictory. Miller said he began to write in the thirties because he found life totally irrational in a world "where people were starving on the street corners and we were burning wheat in the West." He sees the writer as an outsider, crying aloud, "Life should be better than this!"

Outsider, rebel, observer, nonparticipant, protester, innocent bystander, lyricist, a pawn on the global chessboard, the poets and writers may hold divergent views of themselves, but hardly a one today claims a role of propagandist, mover and shaper, demagogue, leader.

The problem seems to be how to deal with the enormity of sensory data bombarding the writer in this torn and ravaged world. Especially and specifically for the poet, I think it is an aesthetic issue: how to deal with the incredible ingenuity of man's inhumanity to man; how to write tellingly and intimately about modern-day acts of depravity so grotesque, so exquisitely cruel that the deranged Roman emperors and the fifteenth-century Borgias look like mere juvenile delinquents by comparison. How do you make a poem that speaks of social justice when, nightly on television, we are treated to scenes of carnage in Bosnia or Rwanda, eyewitness accounts of rapes and dismemberments, and tortures so extreme that crucifixion would appear by comparison a blessed death?

Milosz, who survived the Nazi occupation of Poland and served as a diplomat under the Communist regime before defecting to the United States, addresses this issue in his Charles Eliot Norton lectures at Harvard. He talks about the transformation in Polish poetry from its pre-1939 identification with other European cultures to its "encounter with the hell of the twentieth century, not hell's first circle, but a much deeper one." In the war years, Milosz explains, poetry went underground. Since a poem can usually be contained on one page, it was useful propaganda, easy to circulate clandestinely. Such poetry, says Milosz, is "blatant in its calls to battle while simultaneously, on a deeper level, it behaves like a mute who tries in vain to squeeze some articulate sound out of his throat." Only after the war could Polish poetry move away from the stylistic mode of the prewar era and find its own voice. What had happened was simple: disintegration, total and awesome – the destruction of a whole system of values "with its neat divisions into good and evil, beauty and ugliness, including as well the very notion of truth." Here the aesthetic problem arises. In Milosz's words:

> People thrown into the middle of events that tear cries of pain from their mouths have difficulty in finding the distance necessary to transform this material artistically.... Next to the atrocious facts, the very idea of literature seems indecent and one doubts whether certain zones of reality can ever be the subject of poems or novels.

The object lesson Milosz cites is the tortures of the damned in Dante's *Inferno*. These, after all, are fictitious and thus do not appear raw, as do the documentary poems of the Holocaust victims. In most cases, only the poem survives and thus is worthy of our attentive respect. The poets did not. How can we judge such art? Milosz again: "the subject is beyond the authors' capacities and rises up before them like a wall."

—w—

Sixteen years ago a book of poems burst onto the American scene with considerably more panache than any book of the preceding decade. I refer to Carolyn Forché's *The Country Between Us*. It subsequently won the Lamont Award and the Alice de Castagnola Prize of the Poetry Society of America. The book was praised and damned in about equal measure, though I think finally the enthusiasts won out. In six weeks' time it went into a second printing, was reviewed in *Time,* referred to in *People* magazine and other nonpoetry-noticing publications. Perhaps our delayed national guilt over the tragic mistake of Vietnam reinforced our political backbone as poets. Perhaps this book was long overdue. At any rate, what Forché did was impressive. She traveled to El Salvador over a two-year period as a journalist and observer for Amnesty International and returned to make a book of poems of her experience. (I trust that our collective memories can take us back to that civil war and revolution, which ultimately led to serious land reform and an elected form of government.) How do you write about torture, massacre, and mutilation, how do you make poems out of details of reportage so harrowing that one can hardly bear to read on? Here's how. Here is Carolyn Forché's prose poem, "The Colonel":

> What you have heard is true. I was in his
> house. His wife carried a tray of coffee and
> sugar. His daughter filed her nails, his son went
> out for the night. There were daily papers, pet
> dogs, a pistol on the cushion beside him. The
> moon swung bare on its black cord over the
> house. On the television was a cop show. It was
> in English. Broken bottles were embedded in
> the walls around the house to scoop the knee-
> caps from a man's legs or cut his hands to lace.
> On the windows there were gratings like those
> in liquor stores. We had dinner, rack of lamb,
> good wine, a gold bell was on the table for
> calling the maid. The maid brought green
> mangoes, salt, a type of bread. I was asked how

I enjoyed the country. There was a brief
commercial in Spanish. His wife took every-
thing away. There was some talk then of how
difficult it had become to govern. The parrot
said hello on the terrace. The colonel told it to
shut up, and pushed himself from the table. My
friend said to me with his eyes: say nothing.
The colonel returned with a sack used to bring
groceries home. He spilled many human ears
on the table. They were like dried peach halves.
There is no other way to say this. He took one
of them in his hands, shook it in our faces,
dropped in into a water glass. It came alive
there. I am tired of fooling around, he said. As
for the rights of anyone, tell your people they
can go fuck themselves. He swept the ears to
the floor with his arm and held the last of his
wine in the air. Something for your poetry, no?
he said. Some of the ears on the floor caught
this scrap of his voice. Some of the ears on the
floor were pressed to the ground.

Sharon Doubiago wrote a carefully reasoned response to the
furor aroused by the Forché book in *American Poetry Review*. It
seemed for a while that the critics were standing in line to accuse
Forché of egoism, pandering, violating the code of poetic cour-
tesy, letting the publishers use her picture for publicity purposes
(she was very pretty), and so on. Doubiago attacks

the aesthetics of an elite culture that feeds off of,
but does not want to be reminded in its poetry of
where its clothes, its food, its coffee and liquor,
its oil, dope, sugar and stimulants are produced;
the aesthetic that a 'good' poem is not political.
And this is why we are such a precious lot, we

poets, practitioners of 'a genteel and minor art form,' as [Katha] Pollitt fears, and why we do not have readers, in contrast, for instance, with poets of Latin America, who have large followings, the political scene giving their work impetus, validity, excitement. Poetry *matters* in Latin America. Here, our voices, our power has been taken from us... so that at best we are impotent voyeurs of a barbaric and stupid world.

To hope for amity among bards as disparate as, say, the new fractal poets and the old-guard formalists is perhaps unrealistic. But all of us who write need to realize our commonality in words and concepts. We share the bond of language; language unites us and distinguishes us from one another.

To return to Terrence Des Pres's opening statement: It is true that we have fallen from the Garden, and it is true that the Garden itself, which we once saw as inviolable nature, is now pocked and pitted with waste and toxic effluvia. For those of us who read the Book of Genesis as mythic, its metaphor for the beginning of life arouses in us a vivid premonition of its ending. I think we must now address this premonitory shiver.

Two Junes

June was approaching and with it, my seventieth birthday. They wanted to give me a party, the grown children. I was horrified. At three score and ten, who needs a big party full of one's progressively enfeebled contemporaries raising their glasses to propose sloppy toasts?

Well, what do you want, they said rather crossly.

What I really wanted – I had known this for several increasingly arthritic years – was a new garden.

That was two Junes ago. The garden they gave me is simply the old garden remade, a thirty-two-foot-square plot below the pond on the only land we have on this hillside farm that is flat enough to cultivate. It has been heavily manured, composted, and ardently tended for two decades. A talented young man who works in landscaping during the flowering season was readily for hire at the end of March. Traditionally, this is mud season in New Hampshire. The snow is still melting and refreezing. Many dirt roads are impassable. Ours was moderately difficult to navigate.

He came, with four-wheel drive, to look the situation over. He whistled and hummed and said he liked working alone as he laboriously dug out and refenced the old garden with five-foot-high new chicken wire buried a foot deep all round. The wire was then attached to split cedar posts and stabilized with a top board to which the wire was stapled.

I say "split cedar posts" blithely. He bought them as round six-footers, shaved their ends into sharp tips, split each post symmetrically with an ax, then pounded them two feet deep into obdurate ground with a sledge.

By then it was mid-April; there were still ice crystals in my old lumpish and misshapen raised beds. These he turned – an artist also with the pitchfork – and amended with even more rotted horse manure and then enclosed in twelve-inch raw pine boards.

In the days before the Enlightenment, people formed their raised beds out of old creosoted telephone poles or railroad ties or even new pressure-treated boards for sale at every lumber yard to satisfy the craze for decks. Carcinogens from the chemicals leached out of the wood into the surrounding soil and inched their way into whatever was planted there.

Raw pine will indeed rot in seven or eight years, but perhaps by then my mania for raising organic vegetables will have waned. In the meantime, I have seven safe beds, each three feet wide, a rigorously orderly space in which to grow every conceivable leaf and root, stem and blossom. The edges can be sat on, bringing everything within arm's reach. Narrow walkways enclose these beds. Because no foot is ever set on the aerated earth they contain, no tool beyond the human hand is necessary to scoop out a hole or hill up a mound.

It is my practice to start seeds indoors in plant cells, individual yogurt containers, discarded Styrofoam coffee cups from the local market, and/or tin candy boxes accumulated over the years. By the end of March, I have overfilled all three of my starter spaces: a shelf under the fluorescent light over the stove, a similar shelf over the kitchen sink, a third installed over a southeast-facing living-room window.

Onions, leeks, and mustard greens, happy little warriors, are the first to sprout. Bibb lettuce next. Then, always too soon, I coax Sweet Million or Tiny Tim or some new no-name cherry tomato seeds into being. Long before it is feasible to move them out to the porch and from there to the terrace to harden off, they will grow leggy and dispirited under the lamps. Sometimes they develop whitefly, almost always fatal. Still, every year I aim to achieve ripe tomatoes by mid-July; despite all my cossetings, I have never quite made this deadline. Hubris is my sin.

Slow germinator celeriac (celery root) finally emerges. A new cultivar of red peppers takes three weeks to edge up out of the potting soil; Oregon Spring tomatoes, zinnias, cosmos, nasturtiums, cauliflower, broccoli, and cabbage sprout much faster.

Traditionally, I've used the top of the refrigerator as a warming area for newly planted seeds. This year I have a cardboard box complete with trouble light warming the soil, and this gives me even more leeway to be fanciful.

In the past, I've played with jicama, a Central American sweet root that needs four months to mature. The ones I've grown are only as big as my thumbnail. This year, I decided to take on something simpler and less equatorial, the lima bean. I started twenty-four lima seeds in yogurt containers. You'd be surprised how many individual yogurts two consumers accumulate in a year or two; I have hundreds stored in the cellar. The procedure is to cut off the bottoms, replace the tops, stab them once or twice with a sharp implement for drainage, and upend them to be filled with potting soil. When the sproutling has attained its proper size, it's no trick to flick off the top (now the bottom) and tuck the plant into the soil. Cutworms awaiting tender stems to devour are foiled. Some of these stalwart yogurt cups have seen three or four seasons' use.

The last week in May, I apply this same method to corn seeds. When the plants are about four inches high in early June, I set them out, secure from the depredations of crows, who annually lie in wait for humans to press lovely new corn kernels into soft earth for them to scavenge. I plant my corn seedlings fourteen inches apart, in a triangular pattern in the lower half of three of my beds. There, they form a goodly block in the sunniest possible part of the garden. Corn needs company to pollinate and ear up.

By the Fourth of July, when it should be knee-high, my corn reaches to my waist. By August 1, most of the stalks are eight feet tall. The patch makes a rustly jungle. I creep cautiously down the walkways between rows, amazed once again at what a handful of kernels has wrought. Here, in full shade, hidden from any peering eye, I admire a large spotted toad on bug alert and wonder if this is the same toad guardian as last year, and the year before. He is truly a prodigious size, fattened, no doubt, on grasshoppers.

May is the busiest month in my garden. It is soothing to sit on the edge of one bed and pluck weeds – jewelweed, chickweed, volunteer dill, wild poppy, and assorted exotic unknowns – from the rows of peas, carrots, beets, onions, and bush beans. It's a tedium I welcome. My best thinking takes place while I'm perched there, overhearing the territorial cries of a vast medley of birds, the lap-lap of water overflowing from the pond, and the companionable rustle of small critters in the underbrush.

Gradually, as the season progresses, I paper my way down the long rows of tomatoes, squashes, cukes, Provider green beans, and, last of all, the limas and corn. All year I save the proper newsprint to layer around these plants, then cover the evidence with spoiled hay. It's slow work but pays dividends later on, for once the garden is wholly papered and mulched, no further weeding is required.

How does this June compare with last June? Both months have been kinder to my shoulders and back. Raised beds are a definite asset in the bending-and-kneeling department. This June's corn shot well ahead of last year's. The squashes were slower to blossom, but a heavier rainfall this year has enhanced their growth. Once again, I am committing infanticide among the yellow squash and zucchini, in order to defend against glut.

Modesty forbids me to report how many pints of Provider green beans, Oregon snow peas, and Lincoln shelling-out peas I've frozen for next winter. I could use the word "peck," but how many of us these days know that word as a dry measurement?

This year's peppers and eggplants are thriving, but they're not up here in the garden. I've planted them instead in whiskey barrels on the brick terrace, where reflected sunlight from the house clapboards and stored heat from the bricks are proving beneficial. In truth, I've rarely had any really full-grown red peppers; perhaps the millennium is at hand. Several have already turned yellow on their way to red ripeness.

My new experiment, cantaloupe, seems to be proving itself. These, too, I started in the house, transplanted them twice, the second time into gallon containers on the glass-enclosed porch, and finally set them next to the corn, the only available option. Even without full sun they appear content. I've slipped aluminum pie plates under the two fattest fruits that are resting on the ground. Now the vines are climbing the fence. Can new emerging fruits hang on?

And what will it be next year? I'm thinking of watermelon, salsify, a larger planting of parsnips. Definitely cilantro, and more parsley. I will pay closer attention to sunflowers; most of mine died soon after they sprouted. Higher trellises for the cucumbers. More stakes for the tomatoes. Fewer potatoes! They are so prolific that half a row would have sufficed. Right now I am awash in dill and basil, but by next June who knows? In case a decree is handed down banning them as dangerous substances, I need to have a good supply on hand.

Next June's garden is but a figment; still, it will warm me over the coming winter.

PART SIX

Interview

Excerpts from a Conversation between
Maxine Kumin and Enid Shomer

Maxine Kumin was born on June 6, 1925, the youngest of four children, in Germantown, Pennsylvania. She received her BA and MA degrees from Radcliffe College, where she studied with Michael Karpovich, Harry Levin, and Albert Guerard Jr.

Her first collection of poems, *Halfway* (1961), was followed by *The Privilege* (1965), *The Nightmare Factory* (1970), and *Up Country: Poems of New England,* which won the Pulitzer Prize in 1973. *House, Bridge, Fountain, Gate* appeared in 1975; *The Retrieval System* in 1978; *Our Ground Time Here Will Be Brief: New and Selected Poems* in 1982; *The Long Approach* in 1985; *Nurture* in 1989; *Looking for Luck* in 1992; *Connecting the Dots* in 1996; and *Selected Poems, 1960–1990* in 1997. *Looking for Luck,* nominated for the National Book Critics Circle Award in 1993, was named Outstanding Work of Poetry for 1993 by the New Hampshire Writer's and Publisher's Project.

Kumin has also published four novels: *Through Dooms of Love* (1965), *The Passions of Uxport* (1968), *The Abduction* (1971), and *The Designated Heir* (1974), as well as three essay collections, *To Make a Prairie* (1980), *In Deep* (1987), and *Women, Animals, and Vegetables,* (1994). Her short-story collection *Why Can't We Live Together Like Civilized Human Beings?* appeared in 1982. She is also the author of twenty children's books, four in collaboration with Anne Sexton.

Kumin has taught at a number of universities, including Brandeis, Columbia, Princeton, and Tufts. She was a Bunting Fellow in 1961–63, Consultant in Poetry to the Library of Congress in 1981–82, and a Woodrow Wilson Visiting Fellow in 1979–84 and 1991–93. Her awards include the Tietjens and Levinson Prizes from *Poetry* magazine, an American Academy and Institute of Arts and Letters Award in 1989, and an Academy of American Poets Fellowship in 1985.

I interviewed Maxine Kumin at her home, PoBiz Farm, two hundred craggy acres of second-growth woodland and granite outcrop in Warner (population 2,000), New Hampshire. Her office is situated on the second floor of a post-and-beam construction wood farmhouse that dates back to 1800. Seated at her desk, she faces a wall covered with posters announcing recent readings and workshops. A needlepoint tapestry hangs to her left, its text provided by Kumin and stitched by her late mother: "In Heaven there are many Projects; Up Country but a few." Kumin works with her back to the window and its view of the barn just opposite, which houses her four horses and a comfortable caretaker apartment. Downstairs, in the house, on windowsills and shelves and on the glassed-in porch, seedlings reach up toward growing lights. It is the second half of April and spring, she declares, is about two weeks late. The trees are in tight bud and dirty snow borders the shadowy brush. She is anxious to get her peas and lettuce in the rows and raised beds of the vegetable patch uphill, between the pasture and a small pond stocked with rainbow trout. In the basement, home-canned cherries, pickles, blackberry jam, applesauce, and other bounty from the garden glimmer along the walls like mother lode in a dark cavern. The freezer is a treasure chest of homegrown vegetables and wild chanterelles gathered from her woods.

Right before our first session at the tape recorder, wearing a safety helmet, whip in hand, she went out driving Deuter, her eleven-year-old gelding, in an ash-and-iron phaeton with another horsewoman. Afterward, she rubbed the horse down with Vetrolin, checking for swollen tendons and muscles. The pleasant minty smell of the liniment lingered, freshening the air as we talked.

s: You're driving horses now instead of riding them?

k: I still ride them, I'm just not competing in riding. I am competing in driving.

s: Isn't driving more dangerous than riding?

k: Considerably, but my body physically won't let me compete under saddle anymore. If you're in a wreck driving, though, it's a whole lot more dangerous than riding. I had a young horse rear in the cart this summer, and she caught her hip under a shaft when she came down. We had to cut the harness to get her up, but she was not hurt. I had a little cut on the bridge of my nose, but I was not hurt because I was wearing my helmet. Learning to drive has been a marvelous experience. It requires a whole other set of skills. It's just as subtle as riding dressage, except that you have only your voice, your whip, and your reins for aids. You use your voice continuously. The young woman who went out with me this morning had never been in the cart before and she could not get over the fact that Deuter responds to voice commands.

s: Do you think the danger attracts you to driving?

k: It may help. I try not to think about the danger. I'm driving because it's a way of continuing to work with and relate to horses that's open to me.

s: I know that there are many poets whose work you admire, but who has exerted the greatest influence on you?

k: Auden, unquestionably. Almost everything I know how to do with the line, I learned from absorbing Auden.

s: You never met him?

k: No. I probably attended a dozen readings he gave, in and around Boston, in his carpet slippers. I worshiped him from afar. Today, it must seem a strange influence, an Anglo-American male. You'd expect I would say – I don't know – but some woman role model. There really was no one at that time.

s: Marianne Moore?

k: Hardly. She was inimitable, in the first sense of that word. And Elizabeth Bishop was just too distant and too classical. But when I was sixteen, I adored Edna St. Vincent Millay; I could say lots of her sonnets by heart, and that was all to the good. Auden exerted an intellectual and visceral influence on me, though, metrically, in terms of rhyme and scansion, and his ability to compress those gifts into images, to make a metaphor of a thought: "In the nightmare of the dark / All the dogs of Europe bark."

s: Anybody else?

k: I don't know whom else I would name among contemporary poets. When I was an undergraduate, I was really seized by Karl Shapiro's poems. In a way, Nemerov continued that tradition of taking on the most mundane facts – storm windows, vacuum cleaners – and exploding them into poems. I greatly admired Howard. He was a pal of my desk for many many years. He commented, often acerbically, on poems of mine in process, and I was happy to have the comments. But until relatively recently when I began to exchange poems with Carolyn Kizer, Alicia Ostriker, and so on, there were really not any women influences. In a sense, we were groundbreakers, our generation: Sexton, Rich, Levertov, Kizer, Van Duyn.

s: Actually, you're one of the surviving groundbreakers. It seems to me that there is a worship of women writers who have done away with themselves.

k: Meaning Sexton and Plath? I got into trouble recently at a Sylvia Plath seminar. It was a commemorative that happened to coincide with the thirtieth anniversary of her suicide. And I got up and said, "I hate to be the Thirteenth Fairy at the feast, but I think we love our suicides too much." Then I went on to talk about this worship, not just of women but poets in general who do away with themselves. People were not very happy with me. The organizer came up to me afterward and said, "I just want you to know, we would have had this celebration even if she hadn't killed herself." And Hilma Wolitzer, who was standing right next to me, said, "What about if she just died of pneumonia?" Which I thought was a wonderful rejoinder. But it didn't enhance my standing, I must say. Al Alvarez, who followed me to the podium, declaimed at length about how Plath was probably the most important poet of the twentieth century, which I think is vastly overstating the worth of two small books and some·posthumous poems. Yes, she was a marvelously creative poet. She left some important poems behind, and it's a great pity that she killed herself at so tender an age, or at any age for that matter, but think of what she might have written had she survived.

s: Doesn't it seem that our culture worships the dead heroine in every aspect?

k: There's a prurient interest, a pornography of suicide, let's face it, whether it's Sylvia Plath or Anne Sexton or Hemingway or John Berryman jumping off a bridge and waving. I think we love those suicides on several counts. One, because it lets us view poets or writers as weaklings who can't withstand the vicissitudes of the life they're engaged in. Then there's the voice that says, "That's writers. They're all crazy." But you know, more dentists and psychiatrists kill themselves than writers.

s: Rereading *Halfway,* your first book, I was struck, this time, by the presence of themes that appear in your later work. For example, there are a number of poems about swimming and drowning, motifs that run through your work. In the wonderful title poem "Halfway," in which you talk about being born in a house that was halfway between a convent and an asylum, there is a sentence that I want you to comment on: "The plain song and the bedlam hung / on the air and blew across / into the garden where I played."

k: The plainsong is the chanting of the mass from the convent, and the bedlam, what there was of it, is heightened by this juxtaposition.

s: Do you feel that that tension goes through your work? I know that you're an unreconstructed atheist, but I do detect a longing in your work.

k: Oh yes, definitely.

s: A longing for the God that we don't have.

k: Well, I think all of us long for a "phantom of certitude." That's what Joseph Wood Krutch called an underpinning of faith in a God-centered universe. It's what the nineteenth century had, and it's what we have lost inch by inch in the twentieth century.

s: It seems to me that you're still "halfway up a hill, or down," so that what results is art that's *forged*. Later in the poem you talk about "iron truths" as if this is a very difficult smelting job you have to do – to reconcile the desire for justice in the world (the plainsong, a chanting song of divine intervention, if you will) and the bedlam, the actual depraved nature of human beings, which you've alluded to frequently.

k: Also, when you're a child, and you see things from a child's perspective, everything in the world of adults is an iron truth. They are the ones with the skill, the power, the discipline. They're the ones who have the rights, and you're an innocent victim.

s: Despite your Jewish heritage, I have noticed throughout your work many references, some reverent, some sardonic, to Jesus.

k: It's all a product of having gone to convent school. Because we were so conveniently situated next door to the convent of the Sisters of St. Joseph, a teaching order, and because the public school was a mile away with no busing available, and because I was the fourth child and the only girl – all of these facts motivated my parents to send me next door to kindergarten and first and second grades.

s: They got you at a very young age.

k: They got me, anyway.

s: Do you have a yearning for Jesus?

k: Absolutely. Jesus is mine! That, I think, you never lose.

s: Don't you think it also partly comes from being a Jew? No matter how far you are lapsed, you're still not part of the dominant Christian culture, and so you long for what has been denied you. Were you allowed to have a Christmas tree as a child?

k: Oh yes, we had a Christmas tree. We had Hanukkah, we really had everything an uneasy assimilation in suburbia allows. But I have to say, I grew up in an era when anti-Semitism was still overt. I remember being chased by local kids screaming "Christ-killer!" In our household, my father always referred to non-Jews as his "Good Christian friends," a distinction that happily has fallen away. Who now stops to consider whether a friend is Christian, Jew, atheist, or whatever? I certainly don't. It doesn't usually flicker past me. Oddly enough, the distinctions that I am most likely to make are between horse friends and literary ones.

s: You've written in many different genres. Do you consider yourself primarily a poet?

k: Yes. I always think of myself first as a poet. I like working in the other genres. I like being able to move fairly fluidly between them. I don't think I've ever been in a situation where I'm working on only one thing at a time. As you can see from this room, it's a mishmash. Everything is a jumble. My desk always looks like a paper mountain. I'm always pawing through it, losing and then refinding things.

s: Auden said poetry makes nothing happen. But think about what physically happens: poetry moves a little bit of ink off the ribbon onto the paper, the total weight of which must be the weight of a few molecules.

k: It's the weight of a soul!

s: Do you wait for inspiration to write a poem?

k: Well, I pretty much do now. I didn't when I was younger and more ambitious. Now I'm perfectly willing to wait to be called. And it is a calling. I've written enough. I don't want to write anything that doesn't feel necessary to me.

s: In the past was your method to make yourself work a certain number of hours a day?

k: Certainly when I was writing novels, I sat myself down and made myself write three hours a day or four pages, whichever came first. Then I would knock off for the day.

s: How long did it take you to write your novels?

k: *Through Dooms of Love* I wrote in eleven months, but I was working seven days a week, and toward the end I was writing six and eight hours a day. I think *The Passions of Uxport* took me two years. *The Designated Heir* was a totally different process because I wrote that as separate episodes, as short stories, almost. I had no intention of writing a novel. I had written a poem called "The Vealers," and I couldn't let that subject go, so I wrote a short story called "Buying the Child," which is the first chapter of *The Designated Heir*. And Ted Solotaroff liked it and printed it in *New American Review*. After that, I couldn't let go of the women I had invented, the grandmother and the great-aunt. They wanted to speak through me. So I went on. It's the smallest, physically, of the novels, the mostly tightly constructed. *Uxport* is much more of a sprawl. *The Abduction* is pretty tight, too, because it's constructed around the events in Washington – the riots after the assassination of Martin Luther King Jr.

s: You said it had been optioned for a movie.

k: It's been optioned *three* times. We may have better luck this year. That's what Deena Goldstone, who did the script, felt. She thought it might make a television movie. My dream is that if it became a made-for-television movie and I got a piece of money, we might be able to insulate the upstairs. You see, it's still just beaverboard.

s: You have said that your parents would be, maybe not appalled, but certainly surprised if they could see how you were living now, mucking out horse manure, because that is –

k: That's what they escaped!

s: Do you see this as a reaction, then, to their desire to be middle class and educated and have fine things? Which is what I gather from all the poems about Wanamaker's –

k: Right. No, I don't see this as a rebellion or a reaction. I see this as a natural outgrowth of my spirit. I think I was always destined for this life. Someone asked a friend of mine how she got into horses, and she said, "Well, Max and I are very much the same. We were born with it. It's a disease." It's an addiction, I think it's in the blood.

s: It also seems to me that the last stage of assimilation for Jews is going onto the land, because they were not allowed to own land in Europe. The idea of a Jewish farmer was so revolutionary; it's what fired up Zionism. They said, "We're going to go and have land, we're going to *farm*."

k: And now they're all blond! They are!

—⟋⟍—

s: Comparing your first book, *Halfway,* with your most recent, *Looking for Luck,* it seems that your language is getting more and more colloquial.

k: Oh yes, there's a huge difference.

s: I mean, there's great skill in *Halfway* and the poems still speak to me, but there's one that sounds almost Shakespearean, written in heroic couplets. How do you see the progression of your poetic diction? Is it more and more simplified?

k: Absolutely, yes. The first book has many formal locutions and it's a much more academic book with Latinate constructions I have been paring away at ever since. *Looking for Luck* is my experiment with the plainest possible diction that will carry imagery and a heightened feeling, but stay close to the vernacular language we use in direct conversation.

s: Was the diction of *Halfway* the language of polite academic people in its time or do you think it was still a little archaic?

k: I think it was a little archaic, but at that time I thought poetry was supposed to sound like that.

s: I've also noticed a difference in the line breaks. The way you broke lines early on is much more formal, very metrical.

k: Yes, later on it gets much looser. I think we all learned from Robert Lowell that lines can be uneven and you can play with rhyme.

—⟋⟍—

s: Regarding your personal relationship with Anne: I know that at one time you said you would never write about it –

k: Well, I think I've dissolved most of those barriers now. It seems incredible that it took me so long to come to terms with her suicide. It's going on nineteen years, and if I can't talk about it now –

s: Some people can never talk about losses like that, they're so angry and hurt.

k: I've written about it.

s: The poem, "On Being Asked to Write a Poem in Memory of Anne Sexton," where she becomes a rack of bone on the wall, that was so double-edged. Such a hard edge.

k: That was the real turning point, actually conceptualizing her in the third person.

s: Her voice was partly the voice of bedlam, was it not?

k: Oh yes. When she was psychotic, which happened with some regularity, she was hearing voices that just overrode her own. But as she says in a poem, "Even crazy I'm nice as a chocolate bar." One of the things I learned from my loving relationship with Anne was not to fear mental illness, not to be afraid of people who are in the grip of it. She was never anything but real to me. Even crazy, she was still Anne.

s: You never felt that she was pulling you in that direction?

k: Oh no. I was hanging on to her, like the nuns who hung on to Saint Teresa's boot tops to pull her back down when she levitated. That was my relationship with Anne. I was trying very hard to keep her feet on the ground.

s: Were you trying to save her in some way?

k: I don't know if I thought of it that way; I was just trying to root her. I was trying to keep her sane.

s: It was a great tragedy.

k: Yes, it was a great tragedy, and yet, I'm still quite ambivalent about it. Part of me feels she had every right to end her life when she did. Of course I was very angry. But I felt she was entitled. I also felt that rather than poetry being the catalyst that killed her, it was poetry that kept her alive. That I know full well.

—∞—

s: Let's move on to a few questions about craft. The first line of "The Pawnbroker," is: "The symbol inside this poem is my father's feet –"

k: Which I tell my students never to do, but I broke my own rule. It's a very self-conscious tactic so it's dangerous, but it was the only way I could get into the writing of this poem. My father and I were very close but we held each other at arm's length. He was terrified to have a nubile daughter, and I wanted desperately to please him. Meanwhile, my mother was suppressing what my father did for a living; she was ashamed of it. If you were filling out an application and it asked "What's your father's occupation?" she would say to write "Broker."

s: So you had to actually name him for what he was, a pawn-broker?

k: Yes.

s: Did you have any shame about what your father did?

k: Sure, because my mother had shame.

s: Did she feel sorry for your father?

k: You couldn't feel sorry for him. This was a very strong man. He brooked no pity.

s: What about the red-bearded great-grandfather who keeps cropping up in your work? The tailor who sewed Confederate flags.

k: That's my mother's side of the family.

s: He came here after the 1848 revolutions in Europe during the first big wave of Jewish immigration?

k: That's right. He sailed in at Baltimore, a Jew and poor;

"strapped needles up and notions / and walked packaback across / the dwindling Alleghenies…" He seemed so heroic. We were committed to idolize and mythicize him. But my father's family was poor, Russian Jewish or Polish Jewish immigrants who came in at Ellis Island, part of the unwashed masses. They were not to be admired and not to be eulogized. They were to be swept under the rug! The fact that my mother married my father, indeed *eloped* with my father – isn't that a wonderful story? I mean, to think of that passion.

s: It's retold in the poem "A Brief History of Passion" in *Looking for Luck*. In that same poem you talk about Virginia Woolf who married "Leonard Woolf, *a little Jew.*"

κ: Yes, because in a way, my mother married a little Jew. You see, my mother's family was from Radford, Virginia; they were the only Jewish family. My mother played the organ for the Methodist church all the years that she was growing up. She played for every wedding, every funeral, every Sunday service. Then, when it was time to get married, she was shipped North to relatives in Philadelphia to find a Jewish husband. That's what happened to all those daughters. There were five girls and seven boys. She was number six in a family of twelve. Isn't that amazing?

s: It is! There has been such a revolution in the settings in which people grow up. You've written a lot of what you call tribal poems, poems about the family. How do you think the family is actually faring in the twentieth century?

κ: Not very well. I think the family as a unit has almost disintegrated, sad to say, which maybe makes our family more precious in my sight.

s: Once your children got older, you began to focus more on your relationship with animals and the land in your poems.

κ: They're my tribe. There's no empty nest here. This nest gets fuller and fuller!

s: Two humans, four horses, two barn cats, two dogs, and at various times lambs, ponies, calves –

K: Well, we have ewes in the summer that my weaver friends leave here when the lambs are ready to wean. They come here for a few months.

S: You've written more than one poem about raising lambs for slaughter. In "How It Goes On," for example, you acknowledge the "dark particular bent of our hungers" – that we have dominion over the animals, that we can even kill and devour them. You've really gone some distance from that view.

K: I have, yes. I don't call myself a vegetarian just because it's too awkward. I always say, "Well, I don't eat a lot of animal protein, but I'll eat anything that you're serving." But for my own life, I can do very well without it. And I cannot bring myself to raise animals for the table. But as you can see, this house is full of sheepskins from the lambs we raised for slaughter. We also raised Scotch Highland cattle for the table. But I can't be in the business of raising animals and killing them.

S: Your last lamb poem, "Taking the Lambs to Market" ends with,

> Amos, who custom cuts and double wraps
> in white butcher paper whatever we named,
> fed, scratched behind the ear, deserves our praise:
>
> a decent man who blurs the line of sight
> between our conscience and our appetite.

K: It's written in the first-person plural because I wanted to embrace all those people who are raising meat for market.

S: And despite the way it looks on the page, it is a sonnet, isn't it, even though its presented as simple couplets? Yes, I think the poem's strength comes from the fact that you embrace all of us there and don't condemn him, either.

K: I confess I never thought of it as a sonnet, though it is fourteen lines. Well I'm realistic enough to know that I cannot change the eating habits of the population. But I can certainly lobby for the humane raising and slaughter of livestock. Actually, around here, people who raise a calf or a couple of pigs or five or six lambs for the table take much better care of them than agribusiness. The factory-raising of animals is atrocious. What they do to chickens is just awful. Concentration-camp chicken. It would be quite ironic to raise animals for slaughter at this point, seeing as how both our dogs are rescues and this whole breeding farm developed out of two rescued horses. Deuter's mother we called Jenny Banana, but her real name was Medas Genesis. She was a Standardbred mare who had fallen on very bad times, and we went in and got her. We've had ten, eleven foals, many of whom have gone on to careers elsewhere. I know where virtually all of them are. I'm always terribly careful when I sell a horse.

s: Oh, it's like selling a child.

k: Yes, it really is.

s: I feel that way about poems when I send them out, don't you? I want them to have a good home.

k: Yes.

s: Why do you think this culture does not respect poetry as a serious literary art, at least in the popular mind? If you say you're a poet, people think you're nuts, they feel sorry for you –

k: Or they say, "Oh, have you ever published anything?" Would they ask a surgeon, "Have you ever operated on anyone?" I usually say we have a farm and we raise horses. Then they're full of questions that are easy to answer.

s: People used to love poetry. People used to read poetry aloud.

k: But now we have television.

s: Would you agree that stand-up comedy is related to poetry? To me it's the closest thing that isn't a literary art. It captures the moment –

k: There's closure all the time.

s: There's a lot of closure and there's a lot of "aha."

K: That's true. That's a very good point. But I think one of the reasons poetry is so little respected in the culture is that it's too difficult. People can pretend to listen to music. They can go to ballet and watch it or doze, and they can go to art galleries and museums and look at the pictures, all the while carrying on some other conversation in their heads, coasting. But you cannot coast on a poem.

S: Don't you think more people would enjoy it if they read it? I think they've been taught to hate it in secondary school. They never get past Robert Frost, if they get that far.

K: Yes, and a lot of those really good Frost poems are ruined by creeping exegesis.

S: I think what ruins literature for many people is criticism that approaches literature as a puzzle the reader must solve, and which is predicated on the belief that the writer figures everything out before she or he writes –

K: Whereas actually you write to find out what you're thinking and feeling!

S: You majored in history and literature.

K: Right, which is all substantive information, and I loved it. Oh god, history was an enchantment! I look back on those four years at Radcliffe and realize how lucky I was that I went there. It was such an affirming experience for me to come out of this middle-class, materialistic environment, with its emphasis on clothes and knowing the right people, and suddenly to find myself in a community of similarly focused young women who also memorized poetry on the sly. We were all closet poets. We used to sit on the roof of Cabot Hall Sunday evening and spout poems to one another by the hour. By the hour! It was marvelous. I felt as though my whole life was starting. That's what my four years in college were.

S: Have there been other times when you felt your life was starting?

K: A smaller epiphany, I think, when I started seriously writing poetry. That marvelous identification with George Starbuck,

209

and John, Anne... That was a whole new beginning, to have poet friends.

s: That was after a hiatus of about ten years?

k: More than that.

—m—

q: You're traveling a lot these days. Do you enjoy giving workshops?

k: Yes, I do. Sometimes it's just magic. I just did one in Texas, at The Institute for the Humanities, which is the brainchild of a retired psychoanalyst, Harry Wilmer, who invented and established it in Salado, a town of 2,000. The little white clapboard meetinghouse looks as though it was transported board by board from New England. Forty people came. They had to pay a lot of money. I was afraid it was going to be awful, but it just caught fire.

s: What was the workshop titled?

k: "Elegy as a Vehicle for Individuation!"

s: It sounds like EST or something – an attempt to integrate poetry into self-help or recovery or transcendence, or some other more recognizable goal.

k: I talked loosely and lightly with many examples about what I considered to be the elegiac nature of poetry, its natural focus. After lunch, they all sat down and wrote elegies. And some of the work that came out of there was astonishing.

s: So poetry is a way of dealing with death?

k: Yes. And it's a way of dealing with love, because implicit in love is loss of love, either through unrequital, death, separation, or whatever. Most contemporary poetry contains that theme, either explicitly or implicitly. That's what we're singing about all the time. And we sing in order to save it.

s: To save it or to save us?

k: To save the love that was and thereby save ourselves. So I do see poetry as essentially elegiac, even though there are poems of celebration, there are epic poems, narrative poems, heroic poems, but most poems are about loss.

s: Were these people already writing poetry?

k: Most of them were not. These were adult women and men – a retired minister, a musician, a couple of students from the University of Texas in Austin, some faculty from Southwestern University. Also, lots of people who seemed very much outside the mainstream. I call them "Solitaries," people who read poetry and love poetry and want to talk about poetry. Many had never tried to write before. When I teach that kind of a workshop, I talk about the three touchstones of the poem: chronology, geography, and furniture – the things you need to put in every poem. So that gave them something to hang on to.

s: This in the belief that a poem should be accessible to the reader?

k: Right.

s: When you teach workshops, what is your expectation for the students – that they will become poets?

k: No. That they will read poetry with more empathy and be motivated to seek out more poets and that if they find a poem they like, they'll be motivated to find a whole book by that poet.

s: Do you still keep a dream journal?

k: I don't but I probably need to. I had this wonderful dream last night that pointed the way into a poem I had been picking my way around the edges of, and this morning I woke with great fervor and went immediately to my typewriter.

s: It's been my experience in asking male poets I've interviewed which women poets they admire, that they *always* name a dead woman poet.

k: Emily?

s: Elizabeth Bishop. Right now it's Elizabeth Bishop.

k: Oh now we've progressed from Emily to Elizabeth.

s: Do you feel comfortable calling yourself a feminist?

K: Absolutely.

S: I once pressed a "major American poet" to name just one living woman poet whose work he admired, and he said, "No, I don't think any of them are mature enough."

K: Can you imagine the arrogance behind that remark?

S: Alice Walker gave a reading and urged every woman present thusly: "Each one save one," – meaning each woman writer save another woman writer from anonymity. Then I read what you said recently about the male version of that, which is "Each one shoot one."

K: Well, it has been my experience over many long years of going to writers' conferences and poetry festivals that women poets behave very differently from the male icons who show up at these things. I've seen it over and over. I have so many horror stories to tell you, it's hard to pick and choose.

S: Well, let's have a couple.

K: At a university where I succeeded one particular poet, in our shared desk I came upon a plaintive note from a young woman he had been seeing: "I've tried to call you. Why don't you answer my letters?"; and her first book, signed to him with "Undying Affection," was in the wastebasket. And I thought, not only was it cruel, but it was pretty gauche to leave a trail behind that someone could pick up. He could have carried the evidence off to the airport and disposed of it there. At Bread Loaf I had a somewhat similar experience. An extremely highly regarded male poet was running a workshop and he took up a poem written by an English teacher of middle years and read it aloud to the group and then said, "Now, this poem is shit." The next day he looked around the room and said, "Where is the lady whose poem I said was shit? Oh, she went home. Too bad," and sailed right on. I wonder what rapacious need this fills for these guys, because I have to say in all candor, I have never seen a woman do this. Is this only gender determined, or is it something else? Is this simply testosterone? What are we looking at?

s: Misogyny?

k: Maybe misogyny is the other side of testosterone.

s: Yes, I think that men are actually unaware that if the subject matter doesn't speak to them, they do not attempt to stretch. For example, you and I can make the stretch and appreciate a baseball poem. We speak their language. Do you think that they speak ours at all yet? You're shaking your head.

k: I'm shaking my head – with certain single exceptions. I have to say there have been some marvelous crossovers. Tony Hecht adored Alicia Ostriker's work and said so. Nemerov praised several young women poets. Stanley Kunitz has been a bulwark for young women, from Maxine Kumin to Marie Howe on down. There's a whole list of women who could pay homage to Stanley Kunitz. He is able to make the stretch. There are some who can and do, and there are others who simply don't.

s: In reply to an article by Joseph Epstein in the *Associated Writing Programs Chronicle* declaring poetry to be dead, you said that half the world doesn't know how the other half lives. What's the remedy for that?

k: I guess the remedy is more social intercourse across the lines, more of the women's group at PEN for example, the outreach into other cultures. They have been setting up symposia in other countries trying to speak to women writers in other cultures. That kind of cross-fertilization, I think, is the only answer.

s: What about the notion, often put forward these days, that "poetry shouldn't rhyme anymore because the world doesn't rhyme"?

k: That's a ridiculous and totally indefensible position to take. Are we supposed to stop singing lyrics of songs that rhyme then, because the world doesn't rhyme anymore?

s: I don't know if the world *ever* rhymed. I'm not going to postulate that angst so freely.

k: Now there's a great resurgence in formalism. I think people who can work in rhyme and meter do, and those who can't, don't. It doesn't mean that one is better than the other.

s: The fashion for form seems to wax and wane. I'm thinking of James Wright, who disguised the formal aspects of his later work so that you were reading a sonnet but you didn't know it. What do you make of that?

к: Don't you think that's the playful element, to disguise?

s: Perhaps he thought it was old-fashioned to keep writing in form, so he made the poems look like free verse. I sometimes look at your poems and think "Now, what is her scheme here?" Because I know you usually have one.

к: Yes.

s: How does form help you to write poems? Is it a prod to make you tighten things down? Does it put a little torque at the end of each line?

к: No, it's an enabler. Form enables me to write the poem. It gives me permission to write the poem, to get at the truths.

s: So is it a sort of armature on which you drape –

к: Yes. And I may keep it or knock it out or throw it away. Or crank it down.

s: It seems we're losing the concept of "people of letters" and that specializing seems to be viewed as the way to be a serious writer. I think most MFA students have to choose between prose or poetry.

к: To me writing is all of a piece. We shouldn't have to be compartmentalized this way. Certainly we are adequate to the task of reading both poetry and prose; why not writing both?

s: What do you make of the exponential increase of writing programs?

к: I think they've got hold of something that is marketable. I think it's that simple. There are 254 MFA programs now. Isn't that astonishing? Now it's just self-protective: everybody has to have a program. Well, I don't see anything wrong with the proliferation. For one thing, it's going to make much more receptive readers down the line. And it keeps students out of the job market for a year or two, which is great.

s: Do you see any downside in terms of what's being written and published?

k: Well, I see a lot of workshop poetry. I'm sure you do, too. It feels processed, passed through the mill.

s: The McPoem.

k: The McPoem. You know, Joe Parisi, the editor of *Poetry,* talks about this in his article called "Dear Heartsick" in *TriQuarterly.* He says, why does it matter? Ninety-nine percent of the art produced in any age turns out not to be immortal. One percent will last. So what's wrong with having all these practitioners in the art, even if they are mediocre? And I tend to agree. I've never been an elitist. If people enjoy some sort of gratification through poeticizing, then that's marvelous. They're not out dropping bombs or building them.

s: You once told me that you had a strange fan who came to your readings –

k: She still does. My hostile fan. She's loyal but crazy.

s: She stands up at your readings and yells, "You're an imposter. You're not the real Maxine Kumin." What happens after that?

k: She leaves in a huff. And then she mails me copies of my books with sharp instruments attached to them, knives and things like that.

s: Does this frighten you?

k: Yes, it does. But I haven't seen her in a couple of years. I'm hoping she's back in the mental hospital. That's my ardent wish. But last year I did get several communiqués from her.

s: With sharp instruments attached?

k: I haven't had a sharp instrument in probably five or six years. So maybe she's on good medication.

s: Do you have any other fan stories?

k: There was the drunken priest at Boston College who got up and recited my poem along with me. And my son Dan was there and he said, "Ma, that was God's own drunk!"

s: Do you think in general poets in this country support and applaud each other or are they too busy competing?

k: I think for the most part they're too busy competing, quite frankly, although I've had some very warm, good, experiences with other poets – Grace Paley, Henry Taylor, Lucille Clifton, Bill Matthews, Michael Harper. There are a lot of poets that I've gotten along with extremely well.

s: Looking back over your writing career, do you have favorite works?

k: To be honest, my favorite work is usually what I'm working on. Otherwise, why would I be doing it?

s: Is there any form that you have worked in without success?

k: Long ago Anne Sexton and I tried to write a play together. It was not successful. I found it very defeating to try to put words into the mouths of characters.

s: Do you see the writing process as an obstacle course, as many writers do: the obstacle of the blank sheet of paper, of getting published, of promotion, of bad reviews?

k: No, I don't focus on the obstacles. For me, writing itself is the gratification, and anything that happens after is just a matter of luck. I'm writing for my own satisfaction. I'm not really writing for that audience out there.

s: Who is your ideal reader?

k: A person of above-average intelligence with whom I can communicate in a conversational tone of voice.

s: About something intimate?

k: Not necessarily, but often. And often it's gender-connected. So it's a special audience. But if you start to write for an audience, I think you're in trouble because it's a very short leap from writing for an audience to writing to please an audience and then pretty soon you're pandering to an audience and then you're not your own person anymore. You're just a shill.

s: Do you find that the better poems often don't read as well aloud?

K: Yes, I do. Although, at Bryn Mawr, since I was reading under the auspices of the Marianne Moore Fund, I read the poem "Marianne, My Mother, and Me," from *Nurture,* which is a long, long, poem. Everybody just loved it. It has not been a part of my reading repertoire, so I was very gratified to see that an audience could hear it and follow it.

S: Maybe longer difficult poems are better for the audience than shorter difficult poems, such as your poem "Progress," because there's more time to get into the spirit of the poem.

K: Yes, I think that's true. "Progress" is more of an ideational poem. Lately, I've been reading "Hay," which is quite long. It seems to carry well, possibly because it divides into sections. But sometimes I have the feeling that to an urban audience my poems present a difficult, foreign landscape.

S: You do not suffer from the lost-pastoral syndrome, but most poets today are late, late Romantics without a landscape. Is there anything that you want to write about that you haven't been able to?

K: You notice I don't write about my marriage, or only very tangentially. I would like to be able to deal with it, but it feels too private. I find now I'm writing about my UN daughter. This is another subject I really haven't touched, because I felt her life was very public and that maybe I wasn't entitled. She's director of the UN High Commissioner for Refugees operations in Belgrade, in the former Yugoslavia.

S: So she's in a real hot spot.

K: Yes, and before this she was in another hot spot. She was in Bangkok dealing with the Vietnamese boat people.

S: Any other subjects that you wanted to write about?

K: Well, I haven't written about aging. I feel I'd like to, but I haven't really faced up to it. I haven't confronted it yet.

S: I sometimes hear younger students, people in their twenties, saying, "I want to write but I don't have enough life experience." I don't know where they've gotten this phrase.

K: They've gotten it from their professors. I would tell them that they have a past, they're part of a family, they have a tradition that they've come out of, and they have a moral obligation to begin there, to write about their –

s : A moral obligation?

k : Yes, I think writers have a moral obligation to write about what they know. I just spent four weeks as Woodrow Wilson Fellow at a little school in central Illinois. One of the best students there was a young Catholic boy who grew up on a dairy farm. There were five kids in the family and the boys all had chores up to their eyeballs. The girls got off virtually scot-free. But the boys had to run the separator, do the milking, shovel the cow manure. This kid also had to bring the bull in. He wrote a novella that just took the top of my head off. He could never take part in any high school extracurricular activities because of his farm chores. I kept saying to him, "You have an obligation to tell this story. This is a way of life that is fading fast." In fact, his family had cashed in their chips to get off the farm. They couldn't make a living with forty cows.

s : What will happen to this culture when there are virtually no people left taking care of the land on an individual basis, when it's all agribusiness?

k : I think people suffer from such enormous anomie already. I think we will be McDonalded and Burger Kinged to death. It'll be like something out of Marge Piercy's *He, She and It*, where everybody lives in the Glop, which is Megalopolis, and you can't breathe the air, and you can't drink the water. I have a very dark view of the future as we lose this relationship with the land. I think we're giving up a whole lot more than a Puritan way of life, although I certainly can't romanticize the way of life this kid endured.

s : I don't think you have a romantic life here at all. I think it's a life full of hard work.

k : But God, I love it, even the winters. We had ninety-eight inches of snow this winter and I loved it all.

s : Is there something that can replace the landscape for people?

K: Cable TV? I'm serious. I see this kind of mediocratizing of everything and it appalls me. The homogenization of America. Of the world.

S: Yes, the world because we're exporting this culture of celebrity. Of course, as a poet, you're never really a celebrity, which is a relief, isn't it?

K: It is indeed a relief.

S: Do you think there is a movement back onto the land?

K: A small one. I take hope from the reversal now on the part of a lot of the land-grant colleges, the aggie schools, who have done a 180-degree switch and are now teaching sustainable agriculture, no-till, and low-impact pesticide use.

S: Can you make a living on the land?

K: It can be done, but it requires making intelligent choices.

S: But don't you think people view it as a hard life compared to what they see on MTV?

K: We're talking two different things. I certainly see that agribusiness is going to prevail, but there can be agribusiness that doesn't pour nitrates into the water table. There can be free-range chickens and grass-fed steer and organic tomatoes. We see a growing movement back to raising individual gardens and small-scale animal husbandry. I haven't totally despaired. In a small town like this, practically everybody has a vegetable garden and a corn patch, and so on.

S: But most people don't live in a small town.

K: But Warner is growing. There are a lot of people out there who *want* to live like this and have a plot of earth and cultivate a garden. Give them the opportunity and I think there will be more and more. Little Green Thumb community vegetable gardens in New York City and other urban centers are a hopeful sign.

—m—

S: How are short stories and novels different from poems for you?

K: I think the short story is a natural outgrowth of writing a poem. My personal short stories, for the most part, are the bread that sops up the leftover gravy that I couldn't fit into the poem. The lyric poem encapsulates a moment that you have forever. The short story gives you a little more room to expand into situations and character. The novel is a whole other thing. A novel is more involved, it seems to me, with character and not so much with situation.

s: Have you written any novels that didn't get published?

k: No.

s: You just sat down and knew how to write a novel?

k: When I wrote my first novel, *Through Dooms of Love,* I hadn't written any fiction to speak of. I had barely even written a short story! That novel sprang out of a need to control and work through material just after my father died in '62. The novel came out in '65. So I was writing it in '63 and '64. I started it while Anne was in Europe on an Amy Lowell Traveling Fellowship. That was difficult for both of us because we couldn't communicate very easily. She was, I think, in Switzerland, when I sent her forty pages, and I said, "Please, for God's sake, tell me what I'm doing. Is this a novel? Can it be? There's no structure, I can't figure it out, I don't know what's happening." And I got back this marvelous letter saying, "God, this is a novel! It's going to be wonderful. Fuck structure, just write! Don't worry about it. Just take your characters and go!" That was a very affirming moment for me. I didn't know what I was doing or where I was going. I just very impressionistically sat down and wrote every day. I had no written outline or anything like that, just an idea of the characters and the conflict.

s: Did you revise it a lot?

k: I didn't revise substantively. I rewrote carefully. I worked hard on it.

s: Incisions and tuck-ups in the text?

k: Right. But the story line just got invented as I went along. It's a typical first novel, intensely autobiographical. The viewpoint goes back and forth among characters, but for the most part the heroine's tale is modeled on me.

s: And you did this all on a typewriter?

k: Yes. I was just learning how to write prose on a typewriter, and I was terrified to let go of the first page, so I kept cutting and pasting and cutting and pasting, and my first page was like a scroll. It reached across the room before I dared roll another piece of paper in the machine and call it "page 2." Cutting and pasting was the way I revised before I learned how to write on a computer, a process I have not mastered.

s: Do you think the computer has changed the surface or shape of prose? I'm theorizing that it has –

k: Oh, I know it has. I wouldn't even theorize. It's dangerous! It corrupts you in midpage because it's so easy to insert and delete that you take a lot of wrong turns.

s: You may overwork it, the way painters overwork a canvas. I think that's what I'm seeing – pieces so overworked that *all* you have is a surface, you don't have any translucence, you don't have any way to penetrate the language. I got stuck on one story and decided to go back to using a typewriter, so that I had to "pay" more for each revision or decision.

k: It's interesting to me that you went back to the typewriter, because I did that, too. I'm not really comfortable yet with the computer. I use it for prose, a little warily, and then I print things out and make a lot of changes by hand, and then I go back and put them in.

s: When I write poems on my computer, I have to darken the screen, make it go black! Otherwise, I'm afraid I'll censor myself.

k: I love that! When you're writing a poem, you're always trying to catch yourself unawares, whereas writing fiction is a much more conscious process, I find. Much more manipulative.

s: There's a lot of arm work. You have to move people through rooms and account for their time.

k: Opening-the-door, closing-the-window trouble.

s: Were you writing poems at the same time you were writing the novel?

k: Oh yes. I was in psychoanalysis also. And you're not supposed to be able to do any of these things if you're in analysis. Maybe I'm so counterphobic I did it to prove that idea wrong. I fortunately had a shrink who was not at all snowed by the fact that I was a writer, and this issue rarely came up. Analysis was an enriching experience.

s: Are you still in touch with your analyst?

k: I send her copies of each new book, and she writes me letters. At Christmas we exchange notes. I gave a reading in the Boston area recently and she came.

s: That must have been gratifying on some deep level which we can't name –

k: The mezzanine.

s: The *mezzanine?* Of the subconscious?

k: Right.

s: Why did you feel the need to seek out analysis?

k: My father was dying, and I didn't know it. Or I knew it, but I *didn't* know it. He'd had a couple of heart attacks, and I started having anxiety attacks – I mean, big-time anxiety attacks where I felt I couldn't function, I couldn't face my class, I couldn't give a reading, I thought I was going to drive the car into a concrete abutment, that sort of thing. I couldn't stand in line at the grocery store. That was when I went for help. I was very fortunate to find a nonthreatening, warm, good person to work with.

q: And non-Freudian?

k: No, she was a Freudian. But she was nonthreatening and passively absorbed this outpouring of mine. After a year and a half of therapy, I went directly into analysis with her.

s: How was analysis different from therapy?

k: It really wasn't except I lay down instead of sitting up!

s: And she sat behind you and didn't say anything.

K: Yes, Except she might sum up with a couple of phrases at the end. It's an extremely narcissistic process. But it was very liberating for me. A lot of things were going on that were liberating. I was beginning to make my way as a poet, I had a teaching job – it wasn't a *good* teaching job, it was a crummy teaching job – but it helped me acquire some self-esteem. Analysis just opened me in a lot of ways that I think I couldn't have opened on my own. It enabled me to make friends with women and not to feel competitive with them. Because, see, with my mother, that had been a terrible strain.

S: You said your mother always wanted to decorate you and dress you up.

K: Yes. Which was her anxiety, her problem. But it took me a lot of years to come to terms with that. I felt so guilty that I wasn't the daughter she had wanted. Since I was the only daughter, she didn't have any other chances. That was the crux of my analysis – coming to terms with my failure as a daughter and my inability to go forth in the world and be successful because of how wounding this would be to my mother. Analysis made it much easier for me to relate to women elsewhere and in other situations, without feeling threatened or competitive. Though there were painful moments of revelation, it was not the excruciating, agonizing process it's often painted as. At least mine wasn't. There were some bad patches.

S: Did the panic attacks subside?

K: Totally. Yes. Every once in a while I would feel the ghost of one rising as I faced an audience, and I would be able to psych out exactly what was causing it. The only good thing I can say for getting older – old – is that there is not so much riding on it anymore. You're just so much freer to be yourself. It really doesn't matter what the critics say. When you get a really stupid review, when someone in the audience gets up and leaves, you can survive it.

S: The thing I note about your novels is how compactly they're written, how much figurative language you use, and how many words appear which have dropped away from most people's vocabulary.

K: I don't think this ever crossed my mind until you brought it up. I have to confess, I haven't opened these books in so long, they would sound to me as though someone else had written them.

S: They're also incredibly passionate. And I don't just mean they're erotic. There *are* wonderful sex scenes, which is one reason people read novels – for the sex scenes. But they're very gripping. For example, here's the beginning of *The Abduction:*

> She had stolen him. He was black. He was ten and a half years old. She was in love with black. Possibly she had always been in love with black. Possibly for the rest of her life, at the shadowy intersection of dream and fact, they would be linked, not quite a mother and a son, in a world of their own making. Where the sun always shone, where school did not keep. She was forty-two. She was quite mad. And she had stolen him.

And here, the typical Kumin sentence: "Lifted him out of the charred wingpit of Washington, out of the brick school-yard…"

K: Well that's the poet, of course.

S: Not every prose writer is doing this, and if they do it, they might do it once every four pages, whereas you do it in every paragraph.

K: Well, obviously I can't help myself. That's why I do it.

S: When you read fiction by newer writers, are you struck by any differences in style or approach since you began writing fiction?

K: I would have to say I haven't been. Isn't that odd? I mean, the people I love to read, like Margaret Atwood, Anne Tyler, Gail Godwin, Doris Lessing, Nadine Gordimer. Alice Munro is an absolutely gorgeous writer – one of the best out there, I think. Alice Adams, my old classmate. Alison Lurie, my old classmate. I find their work very enriching, very full. Nuanced as opposed to minimalist.

s: Do you think you were writing fiction as a way of distinguishing yourself from Anne Sexton?

k: No, that never crossed my mind, although, of course, it's certainly possible.

s: But Anne didn't write fiction, did she?

k: No. She did write that play. And she wrote some fables, I would call them. But fiction was not her thing, except when we wrote those four children's books together. She was marvelously inventive.

s: When you were writing your fiction, did you get feedback along the way? Did you have a workshop as you did for your poetry?

k: No, but Anne was very helpful. She was very good at listening to bad dialogue and helping to fix it. I think that was the last thing I learned how to do – write dialogue. Dialogue is the hardest.

s: Do you contemplate writing any more novels?

k: I don't think so. They're a big commitment. I don't think I have the dedication now. You have to be so single-minded.

s: Earlier, when we were speaking informally about your relationship with Anne Sexton, you said you probably would not have moved up here had she lived.

k: Right. I think I wouldn't have.

s: Yet, this is so much your place. How long have you lived here?

k: Year-round we've lived here since '76. We bought it in '63. We used it as a weekend place, as a summer retreat, for Christmas break. The house then was always full of young people. The kids would bring their friends. There would be fourteen or sixteen adolescents for supper, sleeping bags all over the place. It was something structured for them to do on the weekends, cutting brush, chopping wood, and it also meant they were somewhat chaperoned.

s: When you began living here full-time, was your husband, Victor, already retired?

k: No. He first took a brief leave of absence until we got things sorted out, and then he worked as a freelancer. He commuted to Boston a couple of times a week. That went on for many years.

s: Have you gone back through the deeds to see who lived here before you?

k: We have traced them all the way back. This is still called the Harriman Homestead, after an old Warner family. We pretty much know the history of that clan. This was a working dairy farm up until World War II. They only brought electrical power up the hill after the war. When we bought it, the farmhouse was full of dead animals. It hadn't been lived in for eight years. You couldn't see into the windows because the brambles had grown against them. The house was painted barn-red, even the floors. And the hall was painted cream color over that gorgeous wood. It has, as you see, these wide wood floors. The floors and the wainscoting in the hall are all hand-planed pine. It's called king's pine because the boards are so wide. And the barn was falling in. We took down the whole back end. Then, little by little we rehabbed it. We didn't know that it was going to be thirty years of hard labor! We started out thinking of the property as a camp. We didn't do much. After we made the decision to move up here eventually, we started taking a little more care. But we haven't begun to do what we wanted to do, and I'm not sure we ever will. Now we're trying to put this land into conservation use, which will protect it from being built on. There's so much wildlife here, bear, foxes, even fisher cat, a marten-like creature. So we would like to conserve what we've got. We have these two beautiful ponds – one larger pond, and then the little fire pond down below.

s: Why do you call it a fire pond?

k: Because, heaven forfend, they could pump out of that pond. The nearest hydrant is a couple of miles away.

s: What is your favorite thing about this place?

k: The isolation. The fact that it's about a half a mile from any other house and that we're at the top of a dead-end dirt road off of a dead-end dirt road, so that it feels like a little kingdom. In winter I don't admire the alpine pastures because they get so icy and dangerous, but the rest of the year, I love the fact that it's so hilly. My garden, the only flat land I have, is up above. So I come and go vigorously a lot.

s: Have you tried to develop your own cultivars?

k: I haven't really, but I do save seed. I always save my parsnip seeds. I haven't bought a butternut squash seed in fifteen years.

s: A lot of people might like to live this way but don't have the fierce dedication that it requires.

k: Or the obsession, call it what you will.

—m—

s: How important is it for a writer to have a good editor?

k: Probably not very. More than twenty-five years ago, my editor – the publishing house shall be nameless – learned that I was invited to give a poetry reading at the 92nd Street Y in New York. He offered to accompany me; he bought me a drink ahead of time. As we walked down the block to the Y, he said jauntily, "This should be fun. I've never been to a reading before."

s: Do you swear that really happened?

k: I solemnly swear. I've never had an editor do anything to my poetry. To be really candid about it, most editors don't know enough to help with the poetry.

s: Even with the order of poems?

k: Maybe with the order, the format of the book. My editor at

Norton, for whom I have great affection, Carol Houck Smith, made one very important suggestion in the order of the poems in *Looking for Luck,* and it's thanks to her that we have "Credo" as the prologue poem. The book opens with one Indian legend and then it closes, in the epilogue poem, with another Indian legend. "Credo" sets the tone. So that was very useful. But other than making one other suggestion about an opening line in a poem, Carol passed on everything else, and it's just as well. I think I wouldn't have been happy to have somebody meddling inside my poems. I am more agreeable to have them meddle with the short stories.

s: There's a prize being given now for editing poetry books. The very existence of this award seems to confirm what we know: that it's a rarity to have editorial input on a book of poems.

k: Yes. See, Anne and I did this for each other. Each time we had assembled the material for a book we would take an afternoon and sit on the floor and spread all these poems out and talk quite deliberately and passionately about the order, what poems needed to cluster around what poems, what needed to face other poems, and we could then begin to build a book. And after her suicide, I thought, well, I don't know how I'm going to put a book together without her wonderful guidance. But obviously I did – quite a few. I've always been somewhat solitary – I've never gone to any writers' colonies. I've never had the luxury of going to MacDowell or Yaddo or the Writers' Colony at Sweetbriar.

s: Do you think you would have liked to?

k: Part of me would, but part of me would be homesick for this place. Victor is very funny. He says, "You are your own Mac-Dowell." Not since those initial early days in Boston have I felt that I was part of a coterie. I think of all of the New York poets in a cluster, coming and going to readings, etc., and having social occasions. I really do none of that. Here in New Hampshire, we have a small band of writers. Don Hall and Jane Kenyon I see from time to time, and I recently met and admire Elizabeth Marshall Thomas, who is a superb writer. And we now have something called The New Hampshire Writers' and Publishers' project. We have annual get-togethers, which does give me some small sense of community. But I think I've always felt as though I were on the outside, or at least just on the fringe, and I think it's been good for me because it has preserved the fidelity of what I do.

s: What about grants and awards?

k: Well, I am eternally grateful for the Pulitzer, which I got in 1973 for *Up Country*. Harper & Row had published it in a tiny hardcover edition for which I received no advance. The prize caught them flat-footed; they had to scramble to bring out a paperback edition. But I haven't had a great run of grants, you may have noticed. I was turned down for a Guggenheim *seven* times. After that, I concluded that someone on the committee didn't want me to have one. For that reason, I don't write recommendations for poets applying for them although I get about a dozen requests a year.

s: What about NEA grants?

k: No. I did have an early grant from the National Council on the Arts, the year before the Endowment itself was established. No NEAS, no Rockefellers or Ingram Merrills, no big-money prizes, which means I have to do a lot of traveling, giving readings and running workshops and taking on short-term teaching stints to make a living. But I'm not complaining. There's a certain freedom in being outside the mainstream, no one to answer to.

s: Almost all the poets I've met feel that they're on the fringe, and yet when you look from the other side, they seem to be in the mainstream! Maybe there is no center, maybe it's just an illusion, although there certainly is a lot of networking.

k: Yes. I don't know a single poet who doesn't share his or her work in process with some other poet, because otherwise it's just too lonely. You get to feeling rather insecure. It's very affirming to have somebody you can exchange your worksheet with, get it back all scribbled on, and either take the advice or disregard it.

s: How many drafts do you normally do?

k: Well, several, anyway.

s: Five? Seven? Nine?

k: Somewhere around there, I would say, depending on what you call a draft. I do a lot of scribbling. I tend to start on the typewriter, and then I pull it out and scribble all over it. But you know, every once in a while, I get a poem that just comes pure, like "The Rendezvous." But my Jewish, Calvinist soul thinks that you get those because you paid attention and revised everything else, and so the Muse relents. And when a given poem comes, it's with a prickle at the neck stem, an incredible feeling, a great high. I've probably had six or seven of those in my life.

s: If you were to devise a curriculum for beginning poets, what would be included? What are the necessary tools for poetry?

k: This is my stock answer, and it's very simplistic: would-be poets should read in a lot of different genres. I find that people narrow themselves much too soon, especially young people. I'm always saying to them, "Go out and read anthropology, the New Testament, physics. Read in all sorts of areas that you're not familiar with. Get a botany textbook. Try to broaden your relationship with the whole world. And then read a lot of poetry." My approach would be classical in that I would expect someone I was tutoring to have a very good grounding in poetry in this language.

s: Do you think that poets writing today have this?

k: No. I meet these know-nothing kids who don't read poetry, don't buy books, don't subscribe to literary quarterlies. They think they can sit down and words will fall out on a page and it's perfect. They feel no obligation to *poetry*. They've had a little narcissistic burst, and I get very impatient with that.

s: Do you regard poetry as a classical art, like painting?

K: Yes, I do.

S: It's not necessary in a utilitarian sense, but if we don't have it...

K: Well, we have art in order not to die of the truth. I'm very fond of that statement, I heard it first from Ciardi who, I learned later, was quoting from Nietzsche. I feel this is the function of poetry, perhaps more than any other art form. So what would I expect from an intelligent person who wanted to become a poet? Well, I'd set them tasks of imitation. Read Shakespeare's sonnets, and then write a love sonnet he could have written. Write a Blakean quatrain, couplets like Pope, and so forth. And then after they had acquired some historical background in poetry written in English, I'd ask them to read quite broadly among contemporary British, American, or Irish poets, to see what's being written, what's being said, what's being felt. After that, I'd expect them to pay obeisance to where they come from. I'm very big on this. I frequently ask college students to write about their childhood. They're in a perfect position to do this because they're close enough to it so that these memories are still very fresh, but they're mature enough so that they can see it through the filter of adulthood.

S: Are they able to do that?

K: They seem to be, by and large. The work may be episodic, but at least it taps into something concrete and specific that they can handle. So that's one ploy.

S: Would you advise people to read poetry in translation, or do you think too much gets lost? Someone once defined poetry as what gets lost in translation. The other day, I saw a product imported from Turkey called The Sultan's Delight. Its purpose was to ensure that the sultans would have enough energy to service their harems, but the label said: "Will increase the venereal desire." Is translation a barrier to appreciating poetry in other languages?

K: Probably not. I think you can read Neruda in translation, Octavio Paz, people like that. There are some good translations from the Italian, Montale, for example. Rilke has been very well translated. I think our perceptions are far too narrow and we need to read more widely. We're too Eurocentric. And phallocentric!

s: Despite the hard edge of many of your poems, and despite what you describe as the basically depraved nature of human beings, there is a very strong redeeming thread of maternal compassion that runs through your work.

k: As the title poem of *Nurture* says: "I suffer, the critic proclaims, / from an overabundance of maternal genes." I have a very deep sense of affinity with these animals.

s: Let's talk for a moment about contests, which have become an important way for writers to advance their careers.

k: If you remember, I got very badly burned a few years ago in judging the Virginia Prize for Poetry. My animosity is directed not so much at the hostile people who wrote and cried "foul" that I had given the Virginia Prize to a poet whose work I knew. I recognized five or six manuscripts in the group sent to me. I don't see how you could help but recognize manuscripts when you're at my age and stage and you've taught around the horn, and you've met these manuscripts before in other permutations. I guess what troubled me was that hardly anybody rose to my defense. I mean, the poets were singularly silent. I didn't hear from any major poets who have judged major competitions. A few of them, like Mary Oliver, wrote to me privately, but nobody wrote a letter to *Poets & Writers*.

q: They certainly kept the controversy going for many issues.

k: I felt that it was definitely yellow journalism. *Poets & Writers* was hurt that I was hurt but I haven't forgotten what they did. But I also haven't forgotten the major American poets whom I know, and who have awarded prizes to their students, either above or under the table, either by letting them know they should enter these competitions or just by knighting them, and who didn't speak up for me. You can't do this and not encounter work that you've already read, and I was very open about it. I wrote to Bill Smart and said, "I don't know what you want to do about this, but it's very clear to me that out of this batch, this book is head and shoulders above anything else. And," I said, "I recognize it. I know this woman, she's a good friend, I've seen a lot of these poems in early drafts, now what do you want to do about this manuscript?"

s: They could have asked to have another judge.

к: Right. And they never replied to the accusations against me. I didn't see any letters to the editor from the Virginia people defending me. So I was very bitter, and I thought, well, I'm not going to judge any more of these things. And I haven't until quite recently.

s: In "Praise Be," the poem about the horse with the same name –

к: She's right outside.

s: I suppose that the title could be read, by someone who doesn't know that it's the horse's name, as simply a poem of praise.

к: That was quite deliberate. Actually, I wrote that poem as an act of personal gratification and I didn't even send it out to be considered for publication because I was afraid it was sentimental. Then Jean Burden, of *Yankee* magazine, convinced me that although it was full of sentiment, it was not sentimental.

s: Yes, there is a big difference. It ends with,

> Let them raise up on sturdy pasterns
> and trot out in light summer rain
> onto the long lazy unfenced fields
> of heaven.

I know you're an unreconstructed atheist, but here again –

к: But I can have a paradise on earth, I can have a paradise for my horses.

s: Is this really your religion, this love of animals, and the stewardship of the land?

к: Yes, I do see that as my mission, if you want to call it that, the stewardship of the land, the care and tending of the animals. The two things I'm most evangelical about are poetry and the animals.

233

BIOGRAPHICAL NOTE ABOUT ENID SHOMER

Enid Shomer is a poet and fiction writer whose work has appeared in *The New Yorker, The Atlantic, Poetry,* and *The Paris Review.* She is the author of three books of poems, most recently *Black Drum* (University of Arkansas Press, 1997), and of *Imaginary Men* (University of Iowa Press, 1993), a collection of stories.

About the Author

Maxine Kumin was born in Philadelphia in 1925. She has published twelve books of poetry, including *Selected Poems, 1960-1990; Connecting the Dots; Looking for Luck,* which received the Poets' Prize; *Nurture; The Long Approach; Our Ground Time Here Will Be Brief: New and Selected Poems; House, Bridge, Fountain, Gate;* and *Up Country: Poems of New England,* for which she received the Pulitzer Prize. She is also the author of five novels, a collection of short stories, more than twenty children's books, and four books of essays, including *Women, Animals, and Vegetables.* She has received the Aiken Taylor Award for Modern Poetry, an American Academy of Arts and Letters award, the Sarah Josepha Hale Award, the Levinson Prize, and the Eunice Tietjens Memorial Prize from *Poetry,* and fellowships from The Academy of American Poets, and the National Council on the Arts. She has served as Consultant in Poetry to the Library of Congress and Poet Laureate of New Hampshire, and is a former Chancellor of The Academy of American Poets. She lives in Warner, New Hampshire.

Copper Canyon Press wishes to acknowledge the support of
Lannan Foundation in funding the publication and distribution of
exceptional literary works.

LANNAN LITERARY SELECTIONS

W.S. Merwin, *The First Four Books of Poems*

Maxine Kumin, *Always Beginning: Essays on a Life in Poetry*

Sascha Feinstein, *Misterioso*

John Balaban, *Spring Essence: The Poetry of Hồ Xuân Huong*

Jim Harrison, *The Shape of the Journey: New and Collected Poems*

The Chinese character for poetry (*shih*) combines "word" and
"temple." It also serves as pressmark and raison d'être for
Copper Canyon Press.

Founded in 1972, Copper Canyon Press remains dedicated to publishing
poetry exclusively, from Nobel laureates to new and emerging authors. The
Press thrives with the generous patronage of readers, writers, booksellers,
librarians, teachers, and students – everyone who shares the conviction that
poetry clarifies and deepens social and spiritual awareness. We invite you
to join this community of supporters.

For information and catalogs:

COPPER CANYON PRESS
Post Office Box 271
Port Townsend, Washington 98368
360/385-4925 • poetry@coppercanyonpress.org
www.coppercanyonpress.org

This book is set in Berthold's version of Baskerville. In the short decade of his fine-printing career, John Baskerville turned his attention to designing type, refining the printing press, reformulating printing ink, and devising a new finishing process for paper. Unfortunately, perfectionism wasn't profitable. After printing a Bible for Cambridge University he dismantled his presses and foundry. His typeface was rediscovered in 1917 by American typographer Bruce Rogers. Since then, Baskerville has been popular for book and advertising typography. Book design by Valerie Brewster, Scribe Typography. Printed on archival-quality Glatfelter Author's Text. Printed by McNaughton & Gunn.